TECHNOLOGY ①

Eric H. Glendinning

Student's Book

D0940836

OXFORD
UNIVERSITY PRESS

Contents

1 Technology and society

Switch on

1 Look at pictures A–F. They show ways in which technology affects how we live. Identify the different items in each picture.

2 Match the effects of technology to pictures A–F. Decide which effects are positive, and which are negative.

1 fast travel	7 road deaths
2 river pollution	8 space exploration
3 nuclear missiles	9 overweight people
4 less housework	10 global warming
5 cheap power	11 easy communication
6 noise pollution	12 mass entertainment

EXAMPLE

Picture A   8 (Positive effect)   3 (Negative effect)

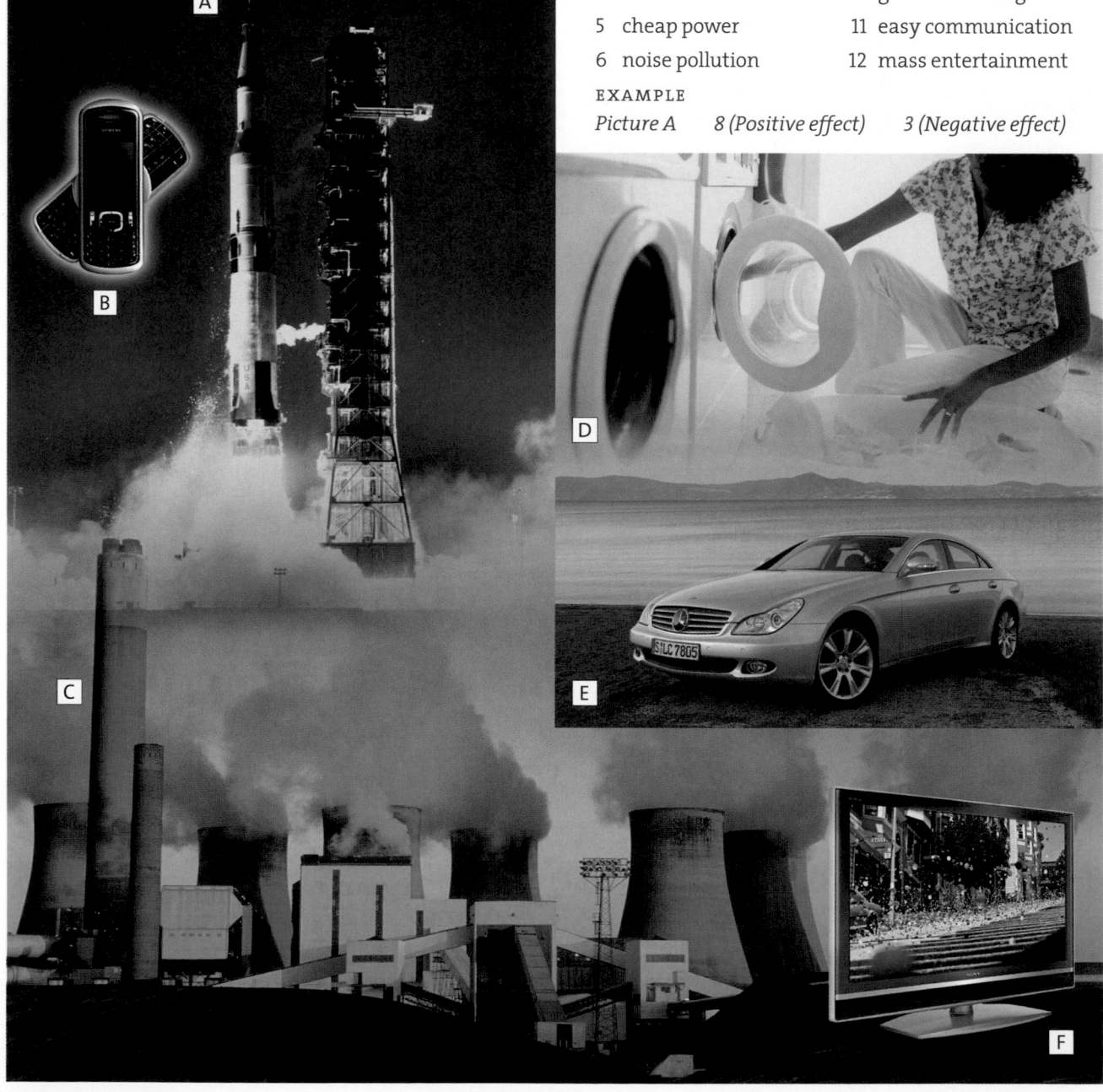

Listening

Technology and work

1 🎧 Listen to four people describing the effects of new technology on their work. Match each person to his / her job.

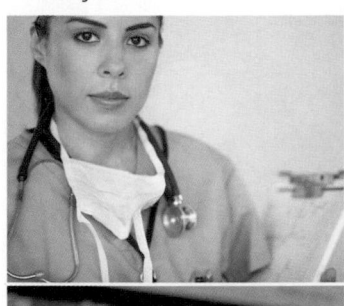

1	Vera	a	shop owner
2	Christine	b	doctor
3	Gupta	c	musician
4	Anton	d	teacher

2 🎧 Listen again. Decide whether each person makes comments which are positive, negative, or both. Tick (✓) the correct column(s).

	Positive	Negative
1 Vera	_____	_____
2 Christine	_____	_____
3 Gupta	_____	_____
4 Anton	_____	_____

3 🎧 Work in pairs. Listen to the shop owner again and write down what he says. Help each other to make a complete and accurate version. Then compare with the Listening script on p.124.

● Language spot

Comparisons with adjectives and adverbs

● The speakers are comparing how things are *now* with how they were *before*:
It's much faster.
It's more realistic.
It's safer.
My sales are much worse.

● We make comparisons with short adjectives like *fast* by adding *-er → faster.*
With long adjectives like *realistic*, we use *more* and *less → more / less realistic.*
Note the irregular forms: *good → better* and *bad → worse.*

● Some adverbs are the same as adjectives, for example *early, fast, high, late*. With these adverbs, we use *-er → earlier, faster, higher, later.*
With adverbs ending in *-ly*, we use *more* and *less*. We can add *much* to emphasize the comparison:
With a computer I can work more efficiently and much faster.

>> Go to **Grammar reference** p.115

1 Fill the gaps to compare computers now and ten years ago. Use the adjectives in brackets.

Computers today are _more powerful_ [1] (powerful). They operate _____ [2] (fast) and they have much _____ [3] (large) memories. Because they contain more electronics, the cases have become _____ [4] (big) but the flat-screen monitors are _____ [5] (heavy) and fit into a _____ [6] (small) space on your desk. Computers are also _____ [7] (cheap). The price is _____ [8] (low) now than in the past. The programs too are _____ [9] (good). They are _____ [10] (sophisticated) and you can work much _____ [11] (efficiently).

1-class (adj) not divided into first, business, and economy classes
range (n) the distance that a plane can travel before it needs more fuel
ceiling (n) the maximum height that a plane can fly

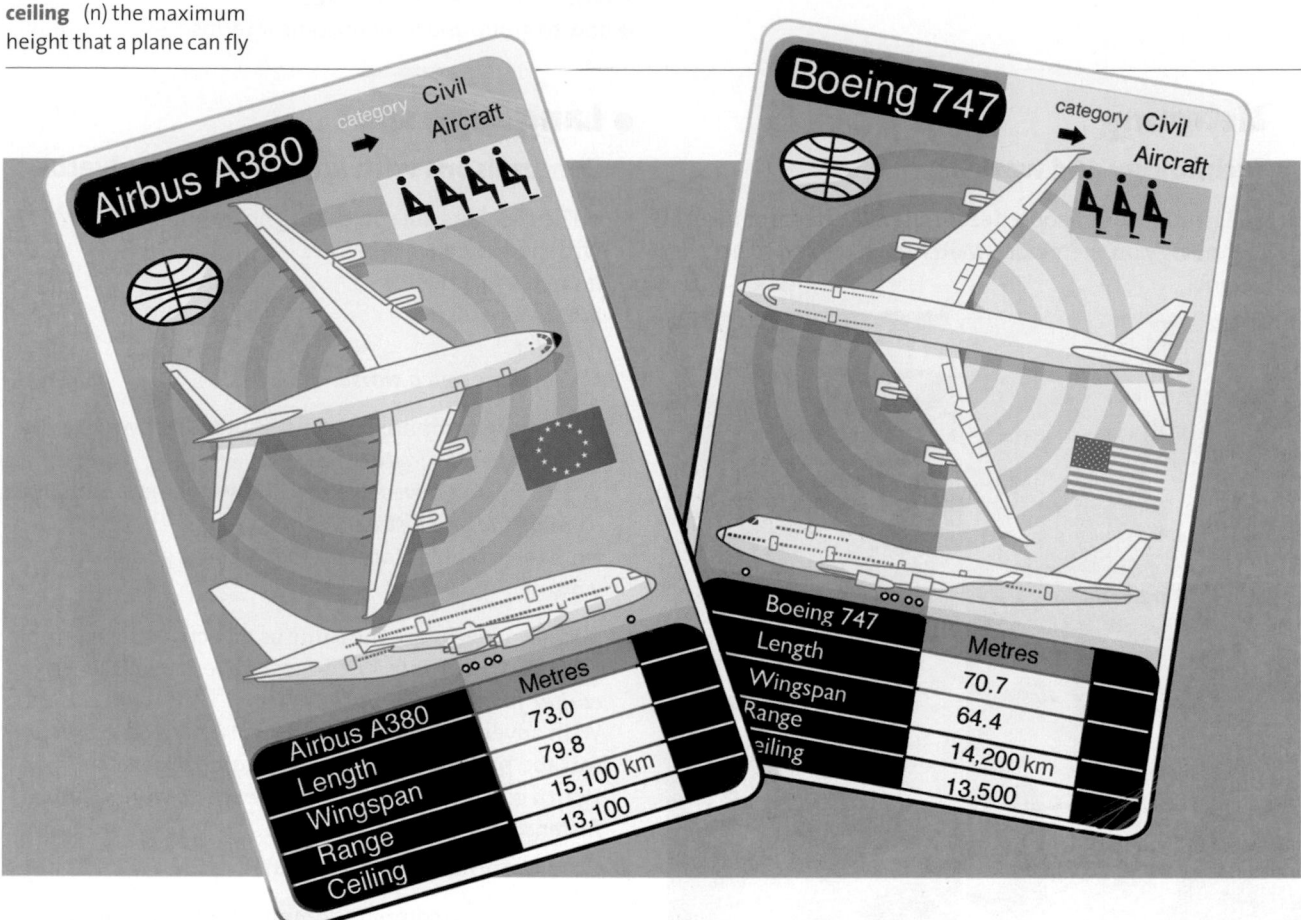

Airbus A380	Metres
Length	73.0
Wingspan	79.8
Range	15,100 km
Ceiling	13,100

Boeing 747	Metres
Length	70.7
Wingspan	64.4
Range	14,200 km
Ceiling	13,500

2 Look at the diagrams of the Airbus A380 and the Boeing 747. Then study the table and complete sentences 1–8 comparing the two planes.

	Airbus A380	Boeing 747
length	73m	70.7m
wingspan	79.8m	64.4m
weight (empty)	275,000 kg	180,800 kg
weight (maximum take-off)	548,000kg	397,000 kg
speed (maximum)	945 kph	1,127 kph
range	15,100 km	14,200 km
ceiling	13,100m	13,500m
capacity (maximum)	840 (**1-class**)	550 (**1-class**)
engines	4 turbofans	4 turbofans
thrust	1,208 kN	1,096 kN
first introduced	2005	1989

1 The Airbus is _____ (long) than the Boeing.
2 The Boeing is a little _____ (short) than the Airbus.
3 The Airbus can carry a _____ (heavy) weight than the Boeing.
4 The Boeing is _____ (fast) than the Airbus.
5 The Airbus can fly _____ (far) than the Boeing.
6 The Boeing can fly _____ (high) than the Airbus.
7 The Airbus engines are _____ (powerful).
8 The Airbus was introduced _____ (recently).

3 Now write three more sentences of your own comparing the two planes.

Reading

Branches of technology

Read headlines 1–8 from recent news stories. Match the headlines to the correct branch of technology a–h.

1 Mice given human brain cells

2 15 billion text messages sent every month

3 **USA developing a weapon to fire microwaves**

4 **MAJOR HACK ATTACK**

5 World's tallest bridge opens

6 **APPLE INTRODUCE WORLD'S LARGEST SCREEN**

7 Sunlight will power spacecraft

8 New ways to make shoes

a biotechnology

b defence

c crime

d information technology

e manufacturing

f civil engineering

g telecommunications

h transport

Vocabulary

Recording new words

One effective way of recording key words used in technology is to group them into **word sets**. Study the example of how to group words related to *biotechnology*.

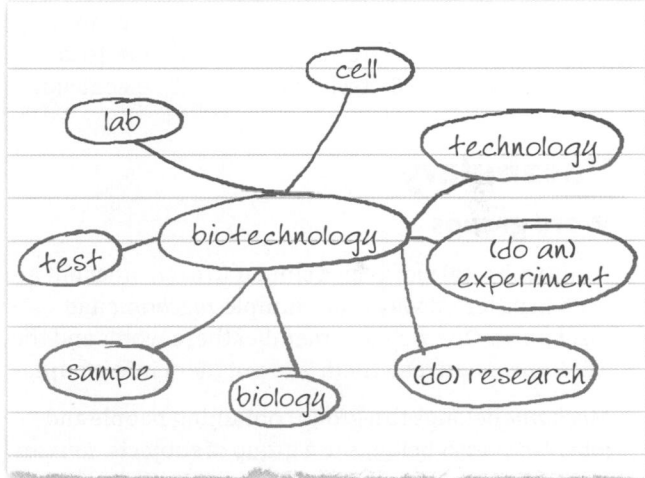

1 Work in pairs. Make word sets for each of the branches of technology in *Reading*.

Another way to remember key words in technology is to make **word cards**. Study the example of a word card.

Information technology	
Key word memory	Translation
Part of speech noun (uncountable)	Pronunciation /ˈmemərɪ/
Sample sentence	Words often used with the key word
Memory is used for programs and data	chip, slot, card, random access

2 Design your own word cards to help you remember your technical vocabulary. Make word cards for six of the words you listed in **1**. Use a good English–English dictionary, such as *Oxford Wordpower*, to help you.

Gadget box

A smoke detector is a safety device to detect smoke in the air. There are two types: an *optical detector*, which operates when smoke disturbs a beam of light, and an *ionization detector*, which operates when very small particles of smoke interrupt an electric current.

Where is the best place to put a smoke detector in a house?

ABS (n) Antilock Braking System

Pronunciation

Word stress

🎧 Listen to the technical words and mark the stressed part of each word.

EXAMPLES   *engine*   *engineer*

1 machine
2 machinery
3 mechanics
4 mechanic
5 mechanical
6 technical
7 technician
8 technology
9 electron
10 electronics
11 electrical
12 electrician

Vocabulary

Word groups

Some technical words look similar to each other but are used in different ways, for example, *mechanic* and *mechanics*. One way to remember these words and the differences between them is to put them into groups.

Mechanic belongs to a group containing **people and jobs**. *Mechanics* belongs to a group of **subjects**. You can think of your own groups to help you remember other technical terms.

Put the list of common technical words into groups using the table below.

mechanic	mechanics	mechanical	mechanism
electron	electronic	electronics	
technical	technology	technician	
electricity	electrical	electrician	
~~engine~~	~~engineer~~	~~engineering~~	

Subjects	People and jobs	Things	Adjectives
engineering	*engineer*	*engine*	*engineering*

Pairwork

Work in pairs, A and B. Each of you has information about one of the launch systems in the pictures. Exchange information with your partner by asking and answering questions and complete the table.

Student A   Go to p.110.

Student B

	Student A's launch system	Student B's launch system
	Ariane 5	Proton M
Country		Russia
First launched		1965
Height		53m
Diameter		7.4m
Engines		6
Payload GTO (geostationary transfer orbit)		6,000 kg
Mass		456,400 kg
Lift-off thrust		1,745 kN

Project: class survey

1 Study the list of the ten most important technological innovations of the past 60 years. Work in groups, and order them 1 to 10 (1 = most important, 10 = least important). Then ask your teacher, and compare with results from a recent survey in the UK.

Innovation	Order
ABS brakes	_____
Air bags	_____
Credit cards	_____
Digital camera	_____
DNA testing	_____
Laser eye surgery	_____
Long-life, low-energy light bulbs	_____
Microwave oven	_____
Mobile phone	_____
Smoke detector	_____

2 Find out from other students what they consider the most important technological innovations in their lives. Make a list of the ten most important for your class.

Webquest

Find out the year of introduction for each of the innovations in the *Project: class survey*. Compare answers with other students in your class.

EXAMPLE   *Smoke detector*   1969

These search engines and this site may help:

● www.google.com
● www.askjeeves.co.uk
● www.wikipedia.org

Checklist

Assess your progress in this unit.
Tick (✓) the statements which are true.

☐ I can talk about the positive and negative effects of technology

☐ I can make comparisons with adjectives and adverbs

☐ I know three ways for recording and remembering new words

☐ I know how to stress common terms in technology

☐ My reading and listening are good enough to understand most of each text in this unit

Key words

Adjective
realistic

Nouns
exploration
global warming
innovation
missile
pollution
power station
rocket
satellite receiver
smoke detector
take-off
thrust

Verbs
affect
download
hack

Note here anything about how English is used in technology that is **new** to you.

2 Studying technology

Switch on

1 Study the description of the course of Alec
Hammond, a technology student from Scotland,
and answer the questions.

1 How long does the course last?

2 What jobs can he do after he completes this
course?

3 Can he study a foreign language?

Civil engineering, HND

Ideal for students who want to follow a career in Civil engineering.

Duration

Two years full-time, starting in September

Overview

The construction industry needs well-trained and qualified managers, technologists, and
technicians. This course is designed to teach you the skills necessary for a managerial role in
this industry. You will learn the latest construction practices and be given the opportunity to
specialize in one area.

Course content

You study core units in:

- CAD
- Communications
- Construction management
- Construction technology
- Construction surveying
- Civil engineering materials
- Drawing and design
- Fluid mechanics
- Geotechnics
- IT
- Maths
- Mechanics and
structure

You can take additional units in:

- Advanced structural design
- Advanced surveying
- Highway engineering
- Quality assurance
- a foreign language

What can I do next?

On successful completion of the course, you may progress to a range of degree-level courses.
Some students progress to employment as Civil engineering technicians / technologists.

2 In which of the core units will these topics be covered?

1 the properties of concrete
2 computer application software
3 forces on a structure
4 calculus
5 report writing

3 Work in pairs. Ask and answer the questions.

1 What choice do students have if they successfully complete the course?

2 Is this course similar to engineering courses in your country?

3 Would you like to follow this course?

Listening

The course

1 Look at Alec's timetable below. Some of the information is missing. Before you listen, answer the questions about the timetable.

1 What time do classes start each day?
2 Which room is Maths in?
3 Who teaches Calculus?
4 What do students do on Tuesdays and Thursdays?

2 Listen to part 1 of the interview. Answer the questions.

1 Which stage of the course is Alec at?
2 How many women are taking the course?
3 What age was he when he left school?
4 What job did he do when he left school?
5 Which subject did he enjoy most at school?

3 Listen to part 2 of the interview. Fill gaps 1–8 in the timetable.

4 Here are the interviewer's questions from part 3 of the interview. Predict how Alec answers them. Then listen to part 3 and check your answers.

1 What do you hope to do at the end of your course?
2 What kind of degree will you take?
3 How long will it take?
4 When you start work as a Civil Engineer, what do you want to build – houses, or big structures like bridges and roads?

5 Write your own timetable in English, including the following information:

● course title
● lesson times
● subjects
● names of teachers
● self-study time and free periods

Civil engineering, Semester 2				
	09.00–11.00	11.15–12.15	13.15–14.15	14.30–16.30
Mon	_____1	Maths	_____2	Civil engineering
	3.1	4.5	G2	Materials labs 4.4
	H.Lomax	B.Davis	Wei Ming	D.Cowan
Tue	SELF-STUDY			
Wed	Calculus	_____3	_____4	
	4.2	4.5	4.5	FREE
	B.Davis	J.Bell	J.Bell	
Thur	SELF-STUDY			
Fri	_____5	_____6	_____7	_____8
	G4	C4	G4	G4
	C.Doyle	D.Cowan	D.Cowan	D.Cowan

18% of engineering students on university courses in the USA in 2004 were female

● Language spot

Present Simple v Present Continuous

● Study these examples from the interview. Why is the Present Continuous used for sentences 1–4 and the Present Simple for sentences 5–8?

1   *You're doing an HND in Civil engineering.*
2   *What's the company working on?*
3   *They're turning an old office building into a night club…*
4   *I'm doing a project on a new bridge…*

5   *I have classes three days a week…*
6   *I really enjoy it.*
7   *I like the maths and physics side of it…*
8   *I want to go on to do the degree.*

● We use the Present Continuous for things that are happening now and for a limited period around now:
I'm studying Civil engineering.

● We use the Present Simple for things which are always true:
*Copper **conducts** electricity.*

for repeated actions, habits, and events:
*We **finish** early on Wednesdays.*

with verbs that describe thinking and feeling:
*I **like** calculus.*

>> Go to **Grammar reference** p.115

1   Put the verbs in brackets in the correct form, Present Simple or Present Continuous.

1   Ms Davis _____ (teach) Maths.
2   Classes _____ (start) at nine o'clock.
3   Alec _____ (take) an HND course.
4   He _____ (study) at Telford College this year.
5   On Tuesdays, he _____ (study) in the library.
6   He _____ (want) to be a Civil Engineer.
7   He _____ (work) on a project about a new bridge.
8   A lot of local people _____ (not / like) the proposal.

9   They_____ (think) it will increase the amount of traffic near their homes.
10   The old bridge _____ (carry) ten times the traffic it was designed to carry.

2   Answer these questions about yourself with complete sentences. Use the timetable you wrote in **5** on p.11 to help.

1   What are you studying?
2   Where are you studying?
3   How long is your course?
4   Is it part-time or full-time?
5   What qualification do you get when you complete the course?
6   What are the main subjects?
7   Which subject do you find most difficult?
8   Why do you find it difficult?
9   Which subject do you enjoy most?
10   How many classes do you have each week?
11   When do your classes start each day?
12   When do they finish?
13   Do you have any self-study time?
14   What do you hope to do when you finish your course?

3   Ask your partner the same questions.

4   Using your answers to **2**, fill the gaps in this description.

I'm studying _____¹ at _____² . It's a _____³ _____⁴ . When I complete the course, I will get a _____⁵ .

The main subjects are _____⁶ . The subject I find most difficult is _____⁷ . I find it difficult because _____⁸ . The subject I enjoy most is _____⁹ .

I have _____¹⁰ classes each week. Classes start each day at _____¹¹ and finish at _____¹² . I _____¹³ . When I finish my course, I hope to _____¹⁴ .

Pronunciation

Strong and weak forms of auxiliary verbs

Auxiliary verbs have strong and weak forms.

1 🎧 Listen to the examples.

Does Alec like Maths?   *Yes, he **does**.*
Is he in his first year?   *Yes, he **is**.*

We use the strong form when the auxiliary verb is stressed, as in the short answers in the examples. The weak form is used when the auxiliary is not stressed. This is usually in *Yes / No* questions.

2 Answer the questions about Alec.

1 Is he studying to be an engineer? *Yes, he is.*
2 Are there any women in his class? _____
3 Does his course take two years? _____
4 Can he start a degree after six months? _____
5 Has he got acceptance from two universities?

   _____
6 Does he have to pass all the modules? _____
7 Will it take him four years to complete the BEng?

   _____
8 Has he got any lab work on his course? _____

3 🎧 Now listen to the questions and answers. Underline the strong forms in your answers in **2**.

4 Work in pairs. Ask and answer questions 1–8 about yourself. Give extra information if possible.

EXAMPLE

A *Are you studying to be an engineer?*
B *Yes, I am. I'd like to be a civil engineer.*

1 Do you like your course?
2 Are there any women in your class?
3 Have you got any lab work on your course?
4 Is there any project work on your course?
5 Does your course take two years?
6 Do you have to pass all the modules?
7 Can you start a degree after your course?
8 Will you look for a job after your course?

Pairwork

Work in pairs, A and B. Each of you has part of a timetable for a student taking a diploma in computing support. Exchange information with your partner by asking and answering questions. Complete the table.

Student A   Go to p.110.

Student B

	09.00–11.00	11.15–13.00	14.00–15.30	15.30–16.30
Mon		SELF-STUDY		
Tues	Tutorial _____	Hardware installation & maintenance R110	Client operating systems R102	_____ _____
Wed	Computer operating systems R105	Structured programming _____	_____	_____
Thur	IT applications R107	_____ _____	Computer architecture A104	Free
Fri	_____ R105	Communication skills	Free	Free

Problem-solving

1 Pictures A–H represent different branches of technology. Match each picture to sentences 1–8.

1 Electrical engineering is about generating and supplying power.

2 Electronic engineering is about designing and making machines that use electric power.

3 Civil engineering is about designing, building, and looking after structures.

4 Marine engineering is applying engineering to take advantage of the sea.

5 Manufacturing engineering is about making useful things from raw materials.

6 Mechanical engineering is about designing and making all the parts of machines that move. That could mean rocket science or bike design – and everything in between.

7 Chemical engineering is about using the processes which change materials in a chemical or physical way. The science behind these processes helps to find out the best way to make the right products.

8 Information technology is about using computers for collecting, storing, and sending information.

2 Work in groups of three or four. Make a list of as many other branches of technology as you can. Try to explain them in English.

Webquest

1 Study the course description and complete the table.

Hornby College of Technology

Foundation Degree 1563: Computing – Web technology

What are the entry requirements?

An A-level qualification, but we will consider other qualifications including any work experience you have. Prior knowledge of computing can be helpful.

How long does the course last?

Three years.

What can I do with this qualification?

Further study:
You can go on to take an Honours degree in Computer studies at a university. This needs just one more year of full-time study.

Career:
This degree gives you the chance to work in commerce, industry, entertainment, and the public sector. There are job opportunities in traditional areas of computing as well as web development, making digital images for animation, and computer games.

College or University	
Course	
Entry qualifications	
Length	
Career prospects	

2 Work in groups. Each search a different site for a course you find interesting. Note the information in a table similar to that in **1**.

- www.hereford-tech.ac.uk
- www.dudleycol.ac.uk
- www.uts.edu.au
- www.ttu.edu
- www.unitec.ac.nz

3 Share your information and try to agree on the best course. Then explain your choice to the other groups.

Checklist

Assess your progress in this unit.
Tick (✓) the statements which are true.

- ☐ I know key terms for different branches of technology
- ☐ I understand the difference: Present Simple v Present Continuous
- ☐ I understand the difference: strong and weak forms of auxiliary verbs
- ☐ My reading and listening are good enough to understand most of each text in this unit

Key words

Adverb
overseas

Nouns
architecture
career
construction
course
lab
manufacturing
qualification
research
semester
structure
subject
technician
traffic

Verb
present

Note here anything about how English is used in technology that is **new** to you.

3 Design

Switch on

Look at products A–F in pairs. Answer the questions for each product.

1 What is it?
2 Who uses it?
3 What do you think makes the design good or bad?

In this unit
- key terms in design
- speaking and writing about design requirements
- how to ask *Yes / No* and Information questions
- listening to and reading about designers describing their work
- using your search skills to find out about the work of famous designers

Listening

The design process

1 🎧 Listen to a designer talking about the design process. Complete the missing stages by choosing from the list.

a choosing a solution

b evaluating

c investigating

d realization

e the design brief

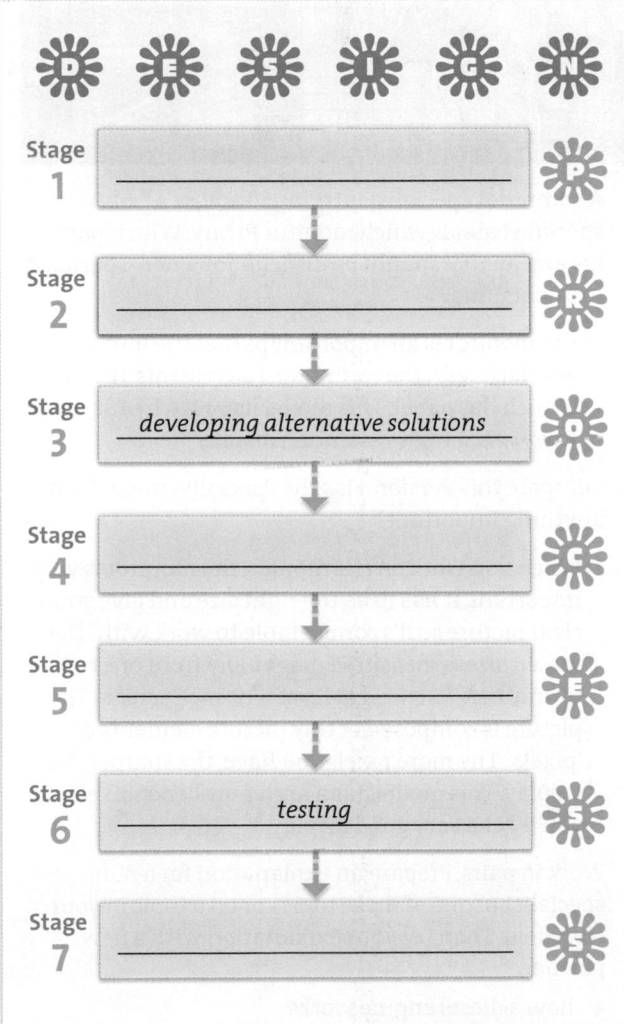

Stage 1 _____

Stage 2 _____

Stage 3 *developing alternative solutions*

Stage 4 _____

Stage 5 _____

Stage 6 *testing*

Stage 7 _____

2 Match the questions to each stage in the design process. There is more than one question for some stages.

EXAMPLE

Question	Stage
Is it safe?	*6 testing*

a What are the most suitable materials?

b Does it work?

c What exactly is required?

d How well does it match the brief?

e How will the product look?

f Is this the best design?

g How many ways are there to solve this problem?

h How can we make a prototype?

i Can it be improved?

● Language spot

Question types

● *Yes / No* and information questions
When we want the answer *Yes* or *No*, we ask questions like these:
Does it work?
Is it safe?

● For specific information, we ask questions like these:
How will the product look?
What materials are available?

● *Yes / No* questions start with an auxiliary verb (*can, do, has, is, will,* etc.) which is followed by the subject:
Did you test it?

● Information questions start with a *Wh-* question word (*what, where, when, which, who, why,* or with *how, how much, how many, how long,* etc.). Note the auxiliary verb and the word order when the question word is the object:
What does he design?

>> Go to **Grammar reference** p.116

1 Make the statements into *Yes / No* questions.

1 It's safe.

2 It works well.

3 You can mould some plastics easily.

4 She made a model.

5 He has designed a lot of products.

6 You design sports equipment.

7 The materials are available.

8 He built a prototype.

9 They've drawn a lot of sketches.

10 She thinks nylon is the best choice.

2 Ask information questions to get the answers.

1 Where _____ ?
She works in London.

2 When _____ ?
She moved there in 2006.

3 What _____ ?
She designs mobile phones.

4 Who _____ ?
I work with a team.

5 Which material _____ ?
We use plastic.

6 Why _____ ?
Because it's easy to mould.

7 How _____ ?
This model weighs 120 grammes.

8 How _____ ?
It costs €400.

9 How _____ ?
It has more than twenty functions.

10 Where _____ ?
You can buy it anywhere.

Customer care
Using non-specialist language

You need a 32-bit KSM, internal NIC configuration, Connexant D110 V.9x modem.

1 A computer specialist is trying to advise a non-specialist about which monitor to buy. Which parts of his explanation might be difficult for a non-specialist to understand?

"The monitor is an important part of the human interface with the computer. I advise this TFT XGA 19-inch flat panel. This model has 1024 by 768 pixels so you get a high-resolution display."

2 Compare this version. Has the specialist missed out anything important?

"When you work on a computer, the monitor is very important. It has to be the right size and give you a clear picture so it's comfortable to work with. The screen size is measured diagonally from one corner to another. You need at least a 19-inch screen. The picture is composed of tiny picture elements or 'pixels'. The more pixels you have, the sharper the display. This model has a high number of pixels so you'll get a very good display."

3 Work in pairs. Prepare an explanation for a non-specialist of one of these topics or on a topic in your own field. Then try your explanation with a new partner.

- how a diesel engine works
- how a semiconductor works
- how GPS works
- how a nuclear power station works

You see things and you say 'Why?'. But a designer dreams things that never were and says 'Why not?'.
George Bernard Shaw adapted by Dick Powell

It's my job

1 Study the requirements in the design brief for Kenneth Blake, a Furniture Designer. Then match each requirement to the correct reason.

Product: garden chair

	Requirement		Reason
1	lightweight	a	stores easily in winter
2	strong	b	spends most of the time outside
3	stackable	c	supports heavy adults
4	available in a range of colours	d	keeps manufacturing costs low
5	durable	e	easy to lift
6	comfortable	f	competes with rivals
7	easy to mass-produce	g	looks attractive
8	sells for less than €20	h	encourages people to use it

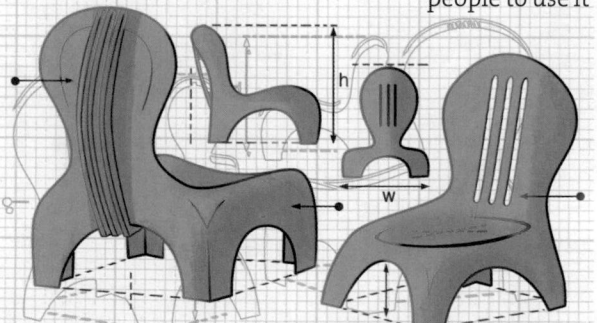

2 Read about Kenneth. Complete sentences 1–6 with words from the text.

1 Plastic is very hard-wearing – it's _____.

2 A company which competes with yours is a _____.

3 A _____ helps to make a structure stronger.

4 Kenneth _____ his designs first and then makes finished drawings.

5 You can make hundreds of plastic chairs from one _____.

6 A _____ is a model which is ready for testing.

Kenneth Blake: Furniture Designer

I decided to use plastic because it's durable. You can make it in a lot of colours and it's easy to mass-produce plastic items.

I went to the local garden centre to examine the chairs other companies made, the rival products, and to find out their cost – about €20. I bought three different models. I wanted a chair without arms so I cut the arms off one. This made the back too weak so I added vertical supports to make the back stronger.

I sketched my designs on paper, and from these I produced technical drawings with all the dimensions. I made a full-scale model to make sure the chair looked good and was comfortable. Then I transferred my drawings to a 3-D computer modelling program, and sent a copy by file transfer to the moulding company.

They made a mould and sent me a prototype chair. I added more supports to the back and the chair was ready to produce.

3 Write questions to ask Kenneth about his design. The answers should be in the text above.

EXAMPLES
Why did you go to the garden centre?
How much do garden chairs cost?
Did you make a model?

4 Now practise your questions in pairs. Take turns to ask and answer.

Gadget box

This wall-mounted CD player was designed by Japanese designer Naoto Fukasawa just for fun in 1999. Now it is one of the top selling products at Muji.

Why do you think this design is so successful?

Listening

Working with design

1 You are going to hear three people talking about their work with design. Before you listen, find out how each of the words in the diagram below relates to design. Use the Glossary on p.131 to help.

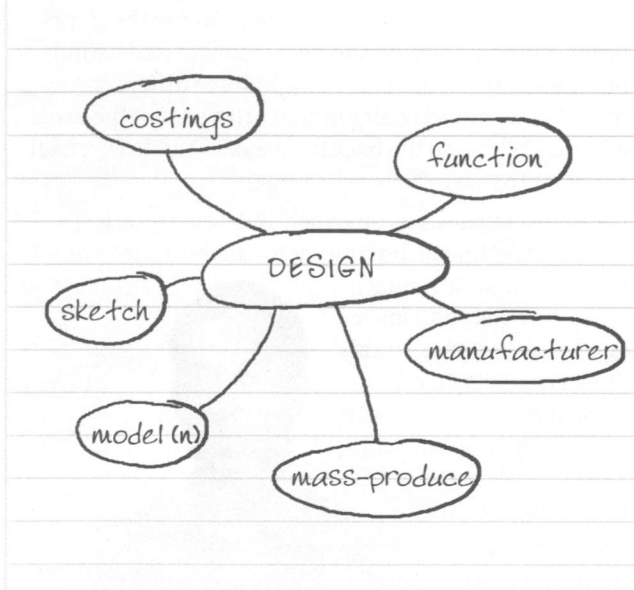

2 🎧 Now listen and note the answers to the questions.

A Karl
1 What does he design?
2 What two things does he think about when he's designing?
3 What does he start with?

B Martin
4 What does he design?
5 What two things does he have to balance?
6 What does he start with?

C Hilary
7 What does she do?
8 What two groups does she work with?
9 What does she have to work out?

3 🎧 Listen again to part A. Work in pairs. Write down as much as you can of what Karl says. Help each other to make a complete and accurate version. Then compare with the Listening script on p.125.

Problem-solving

1 Work in small groups. Look at the designs for chairs which are used in a room intended both for lectures and for indoor sports. List the advantages and disadvantages of each model.

Useful language

It's too heavy.   *It looks comfortable.*
It's not strong enough. *You can stack it. It's stackable.*

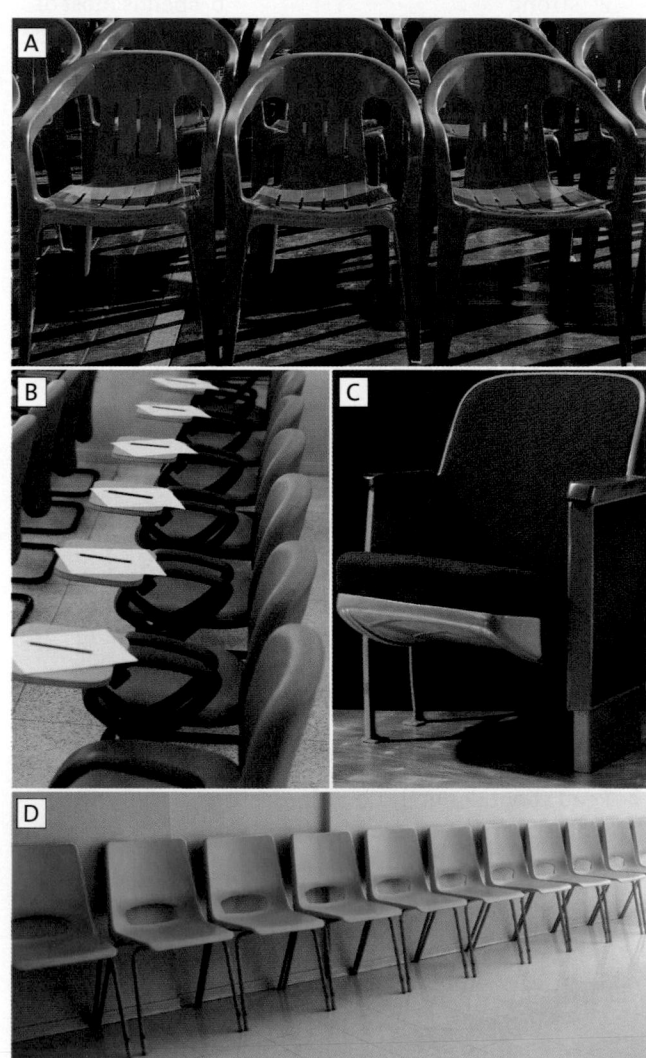

2 In your groups, design a chair for use in classrooms in your school or college. Sketch your solution and present it to the class. Decide which chair is the most suitable.

Pairwork

1 Work in pairs, A and B. Each of you has information about one designer. Complete the table below for your designer and exchange information with your partner by asking and answering questions.

Student A Go to p.110.

	Student A's designer	Student B's designer
Name		
Dates		
Nationality		
Famous for designing		

Student B
Ferdinand Porsche (1875–1951). Austrian car designer who contributed to the design of the first Volkswagen and the Auto Union racing cars.

2 In your pairs, find out the same information about these designers.

1 Alec Issigonis
2 Philippe Starck
3 Giorgetto Giugiaro

These sites may help you:
- www.tinyurl.com/qat7n
- www.wikipedia.org

Key words

Adjectives
rival
vertical

Nouns
brief
costings
function
manufacturer
model
mould
product
prototype
support

Verbs
evaluate
investigate
mass-produce
sketch

Note here anything about how English is used in technology that is **new** to you.

4 Technology in sport

Switch on

Look at the picture of a mountain bike and its rider. Match the items of the rider's clothing and the bike components to the materials in the table.

brake cables	rims	~~shorts~~
helmet	saddle	tyres and pedals
frame	shoe soles	wheel bearings

Rider's clothing	Materials	Reason
shorts	Kevlar and nylon	aerodynamic wear-resistant
1_____	rubber	good grip
2_____	polystyrene and polycarbonate	strong, lightweight – 250 grammes

Bike components	Materials	Reason
3_____	rubber	good grip
4_____	braided steel	very strong
5_____	steel	hard
6_____	aluminium alloy	light, strong
7_____	titanium	lighter and stronger than steel, highly corrosion-resistant
8_____	nylon	light, flexible

HELMET

SHORTS

SADDLE

FRAME

WHEEL BEARINGS

BRAKE CABLES

RIM

TYRE

PEDAL

SHOE SOLE

It's my job

1 What do you think are the most important factors in choosing materials for a bike? Read about Pedro Fernandez, a Bike Maker, and check your answers.

Pedro Fernandez: Bike Maker

When I choose a material for a bike frame, I have to think about the properties of the material. How elastic is it? If you bend or stretch it, will it go back to its original shape? If it does, it has high elasticity. How strong is it? There are two kinds of strength. The first is how much force you need to bend it to a point where it can't go back to its original shape. The second is the amount of force you need to break it.

Steel is the least expensive choice. There's a wide range of standard gauge tubes available. It's strong and it has good elasticity but it's heavy.

Aluminium is light and strong but it's flexible. However, the more it bends, the quicker it breaks. So aluminium bike frames use large diameter tubes. That limits the amount of bending.

Titanium has a great strength-to-weight ratio. It's got good elasticity so when it bends it tends to return to its original shape. It's corrosion-resistant so you don't need to paint it. But it's expensive – fifteen times the price of steel!

The professionals use carbon fibre. It's very light and it's very strong. You can shape it any way you like. But carbon-fibre frames are hand-made so they're very expensive.

2 Complete the table with the advantages and disadvantages of the materials mentioned by Pedro.

Material	Advantages	Disadvantages
steel		
aluminium		
titanium		
carbon fibre		

● Language spot
used to, used for, made of, made from

● Study the ways of describing how materials are used:
*Steel **is used to make** the bearings.*
*Titanium **is used for making** the frame.*
*The wheels **are made of** aluminium alloy.*
*A bike **is made from** many different materials.*

● We can add a reason to explain the choice of material:

Steel **is used to** make the bearings <u>because it is hard</u>.

>> Go to **Grammar reference** p.117

1 Correct the errors in these sentences.
1 Rubber is used for make the tyres.
2 The frame is made titanium.
3 Kevlar is used to making the rider's clothing.
4 Because it is very strong, braided steel is used to brake cables.
5 Carbon fibre is used make racing bike frames.
6 Steel is made iron and carbon.

2 Explain the choice of materials for each of the items in the table on p.22.

3 Identify the main material in items of sports equipment 1–10. Tick (✓) the material used. More than one answer is possible in some cases.

1 baseball bat

	nylon
	aluminium
	wood

2 football

	leather
	polyurethane
	fibreglass

3 vaulting pole

	nylon
	Kevlar
	fibreglass

4 ski poles

	aluminium
	graphite
	carbon-fibre

5 tennis racket

	graphite composites
	nylon
	wood

6 kayak

	fibreglass
	aluminium
	plastic laminates

7 ice skates

	nylon
	high carbon steel
	wood

8 crash helmet

	Kevlar
	titanium
	plastic

9 bobsleigh

	steel
	PVC
	aluminium

10 hang glider

	aluminium and polyester
	wood and nylon
	wood and acrylic

Thanks to the large multi-component core and a cover made of a soft, thin, high-performance urethane, golfers are driving over 20 yards further on average.
Golf ball advertisement

Pronunciation
Intonation for questions

Information or *wh*-questions begin with a question word: *who, what, where, when, how.* Your voice goes down on the last important word in an information question.

1 Listen to the examples.

Where are you from?

What do you study?

Yes / No questions expect the answer *Yes* or *No.* They don't contain question words. Your voice goes up on the last important word in *Yes / No* questions.

2 Listen to the examples.

Are you Italian?

Do you speak English?

3 Listen to the short dialogue and mark the intonation.

A What materials do we use for ski poles?

B Aluminium or carbon-fibre, I think. What are footballs made of?

A I'm not sure. Is it leather?

B Yes, I'm certain. What's used to make bobsleighs?

4 Work in pairs. Ask questions to check your answers to *Language spot* **3**. Use the correct intonation.

Vocabulary
Describing materials

1 Study the words used to describe materials. Fill the gaps. Most of the words have been used in this unit.

Adjective	Noun
1 *elastic*	*elasticity*
2 _____	plasticity
3 strong	_____
4 _____	corrosion-resistance
5 wear-resistant	_____
6 brittle	_____
7 _____	hardness
8 tough	_____
9 _____	flexibility

2 Check the meaning of any unfamiliar words using the Glossary on p.131. Then fill the gaps in sentences 1–8 with the correct word from the table.

1   Fibreglass is used for vaulting poles because it's light and _____ . It bends very easily.

2   You don't need to paint titanium because it's _____ .

3   Bike bearings are made from steel because it's _____ .

4   A material which returns to its original shape when you bend it has high _____ .

5   Rubber is very _____ . You can stretch it without breaking it.

6   Diamond is an incredibly _____ substance. It is sometimes used for drilling as well as for jewellery.

7   Glass is very _____ . It breaks easily.

8   Kevlar doesn't wear out easily. It's _____ .

Gadget box

Adidas 1 trainers contain a microcomputer, a battery, and a tiny motor in the sole. The trainer senses the surface you're running on and adjusts the amount of support provided. It also takes into account the weather, the weight of the athlete, and the intensity of the sporting activity. The battery lasts for 100 hours.

What else could you do to improve the trainers?

Speaking

Skateboard v snowboard

Work in pairs, A and B. Each of you has a diagram of a piece of sports equipment. With the help of your partner, who has information about your equipment, label your diagram and complete the table below. Give reasons for the choice of material where possible.

Student A   Go to p.110.

Student B

Snowboard		
Part / Component	Materials used	Reason

Skateboard

The body of a skateboard is called a deck. Plywood is the most common deck material used because it's light but strong. The front of the board is called the nose and the back is called the tail. The nose and tail are tilted up at a twenty degree angle. These help the skateboarder perform tricks.

Fixed to the deck are two metal alloy trucks which connect to the wheels. Some truck alloys contain titanium for strength. The top part of the truck is called the baseplate. It's screwed to the deck. The bottom part is called the hanger. It's fixed to the wheels, which are made of polyurethane. The hardness of the wheels varies. Very hard wheels are good for performance but not for rough surfaces. Between the baseplate and the hanger are bushings which provide the spring mechanism for turning the board.

Listening

Exchanging information

1 🎧 Listen to this extract from a conversation between two students. Then repeat the activity in *Speaking*.

2 🎧 Listen again to the second part of the conversation and complete the questions.

1 Is it _____ fibreglass?

2 Really? _____ ?

3 OK. Is it the same _____ ?

4 What's _____ ?

5 Right. Important on snow. What _____ the edge? _____ made of *p-tex* as well?

6 _____ it turns and does tricks?

7 OK. Oh, and these straps – _____ made of nylon?

Customer care

Making recommendations

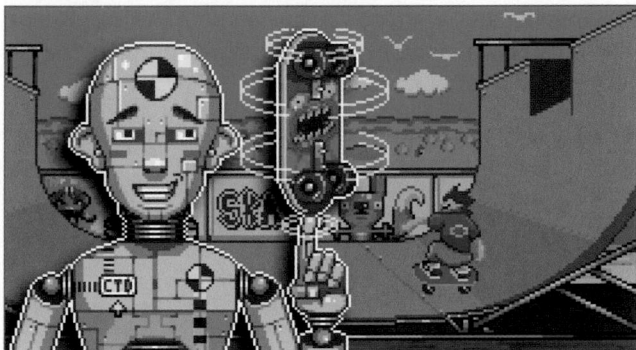

1 A student of materials science is advising his friend how to choose the right skateboard deck. His friend is a new skateboarder, and quite short and light. Study the expressions he uses to make recommendations.

"*I'd go for* a wooden deck – wood is more responsive than plastic or a composite."

"If you're going to use it mainly on the street, *I'd recommend* a short board and not too wide so you'll have more control. *Your best bet* is something a little less than twenty centimetres."

"The shape is important. For a new skater, *I'd advise* something shallow – not too deep."

2 Work in pairs. Make recommendations about the skateboard wheels using this information.

Size	Used for
52–55 mm	Street, skate parks. Shorter and lighter riders.
56–60 mm	Many uses. Street, skate parks, ramps. Taller and heavier riders.
60+ mm	Speciality rides. Long boards, dirt boards, hills.

Hardness	Used for
87A	Very rough surfaces, long boards, hills.
95A	Hard and durable. Street, rough surfaces.
97A	Street, skate parks. Smooth surfaces.
100A	Very hard. Top professionals only.

Key words

Adjectives
aerodynamic
flexible

Nouns
alloy
bearings
composites
corrosion
laminate
performance
plywood
property
pvc
ratio
wear

Verbs
stretch
vary

Note here anything about how English is used in technology that is **new** to you.

5 Appropriate technology

Switch on

1 Work in pairs. Look at the mechanism and answer the questions.

1 What is it?

2 What does it do?

3 How does it work?

4 In which parts of the world is it used?

5 What's it made from?

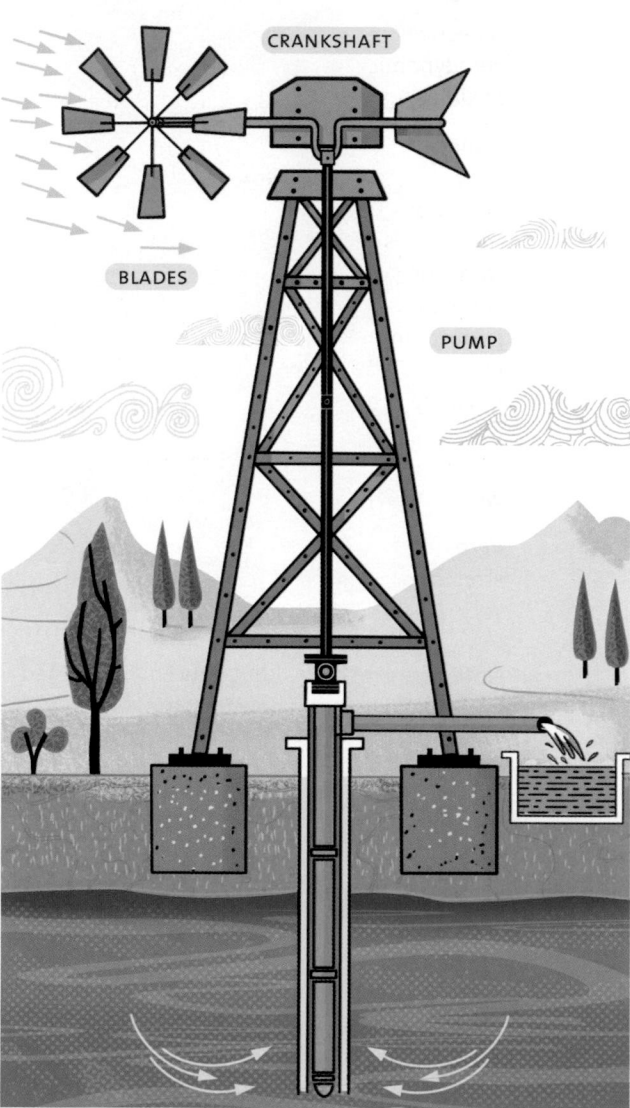

CRANKSHAFT

BLADES

PUMP

2 🎧 Now listen to the explanation by an Agricultural Engineer, and check your answers.

Reading

The inventor

1 Work in pairs. What do you know about the inventor of the clockwork radio? Read the first paragraph of the text and check your answers.

2 Read the rest of the text and match parts a–e to the numbered components on the diagram.

a winding handle

b steel spring

c generator

d gears

e pulley

3 Scan the text. What do the following numbers and quantities refer to?

a more than two million

b 60

c 3V

d 30 minutes

e 1991

f 30 mA

4 Complete the sentences using information from the text.

1 As you turn the handle on the side of the radio,

_____ .

2 When the spring unwinds,_____

_____ .

3 As the generator turns,_____

_____ .

4 The spring has enough power to run the radio for 30 minutes before _____

_____ .

5 The electric shoe charges batteries as _____

_____ .

The clockwork radio

Trevor Baylis is an inventor. In 1991, he heard about the problem of bringing health information to people in rural Africa. Radio was the best way but people had no electricity and couldn't pay for expensive batteries. So he invented a radio which doesn't need mains power or batteries. Instead, it consists of a spring, gears, and a small generator.

So how does his clockwork radio actually function? As you turn the handle on the side of the radio, you wind up a spring. It's the same kind of steel spring used in car safety belts. It takes 60 turns to wind up the spring fully.

When the spring starts to unwind, the gears engage. There are three 1:10 step-up gears. The last step-up link is a pulley. Pulleys run more quietly than gears so this reduces noise. Each time the first gear turns, the generator turns one thousand times. As it turns, it generates electricity – a voltage of 3V at about 30 mA. The spring has enough power to run the radio for 30 minutes before you have to wind it up again.

More than two million clockwork radios are in use all over the world. Trevor Baylis has also invented an electric shoe. It charges batteries as you walk.

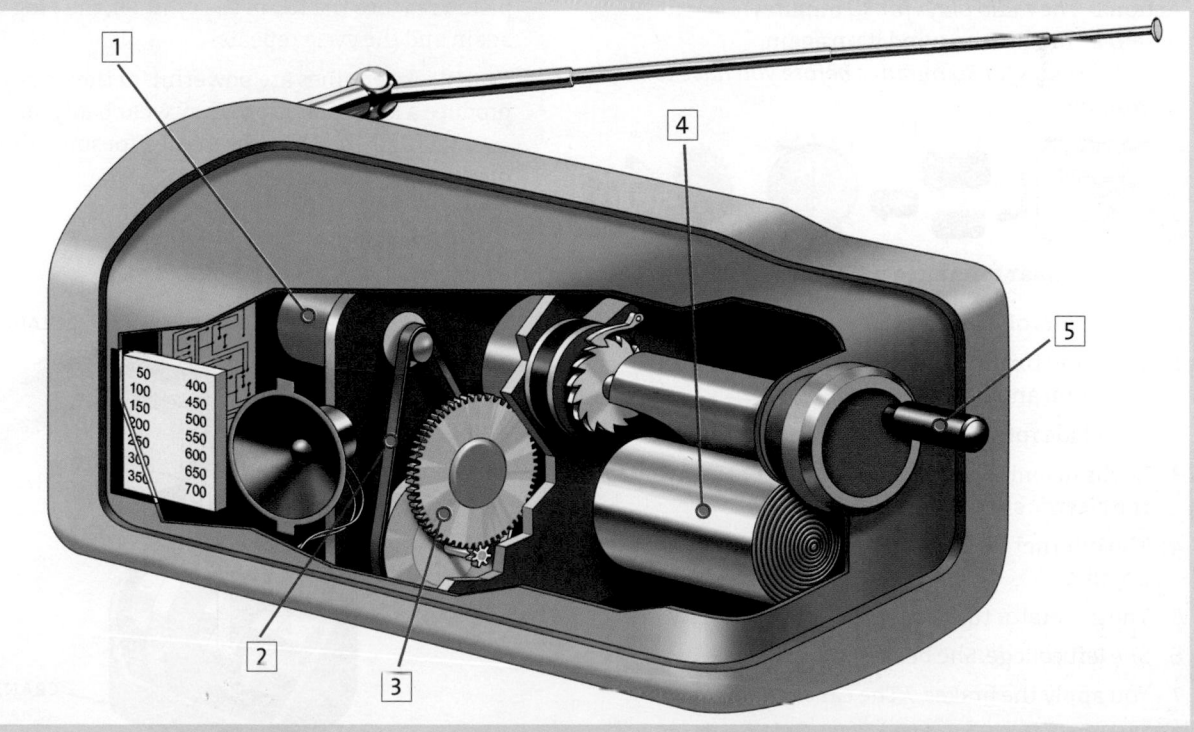

Gadget box

Professor Negroponte of MIT (Massachusetts Institute of Technology) in the USA has developed a clockwork computer which will cost less than $100. This low-cost laptop is intended for children in the developing world. It uses open source software and will connect to Wi-Fi networks. He hopes to produce 150 million a year.

Why does this computer use 'open source' software and connect to Wi-Fi networks?

● Language spot

Time clauses

● To show actions in quick succession, we use *when*:

Action 1 *The spring starts to unwind.*
Action 2 The gears engage.
When *the spring starts to unwind, the gears engage.*

● To show actions happening at the same time, we use *as*:

Action 1 *You walk.*
Action 2 The electric shoe charges batteries.
As *you walk, the electric shoe charges batteries.*

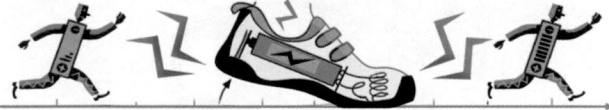

● To put actions in sequence, we use *before* or *after*:

Action 1 *The radio plays for 30 minutes.*
Action 2 You have to wind it up again.
The radio plays for 30 minutes **before** *you have to wind it up again.*

>> Go to **Grammar reference** p.117

1 Link the pairs of actions with a suitable time word.

1 The wind turns the pump blades. / The piston moves up and down.

2 The blade rotates. / Water is pumped from the well.

3 Baylis invented the clockwork radio. / He invented the electric shoe.

4 The Internet existed. / The World Wide Web became popular.

5 The generator turns. / It produces electricity.

6 She left college. She became an engineer.

7 You apply the brakes. / The car slows down.

8 You press the accelerator. / The car speeds up.

2 Choose suitable time words to fill the gaps in the explanation of a two-stroke engine. Use the diagram to help.

The two-stroke engine

_____[1] you can use a two-stroke engine, you have to fill the fuel tank with petrol and oil in the right ratio, usually 40:1.

Combustion stroke

_____[2] the spark plug fires, the fuel ignites. The explosion pushes the piston down. _____[3] it moves down, it compresses the fuel in the crankcase on the other side of the piston. _____[4] the piston nears the bottom, it uncovers the exhaust port. The pressurized fuel in the crankcase rushes into the cylinder. The pressure pushes out the exhaust gas. _____[5] the piston reaches the bottom, it uncovers the fuel intake port.

Compression stroke

_____[6] the piston moves up the cylinder, it compresses the fuel. At the same time, the fuel valve opens and fresh fuel is sucked in. Just _____[7] the piston reaches the top of the cylinder, the plug fires again and the cycle repeats.

Two-stroke engines are powerful for their size but they produce a lot of pollution. They wear badly and _____[8] they have been used for some time, they produce oily smoke.

SPARK PLUG

COMBUSTION CHAMBER

EXHAUST

PISTON

FUEL INTAKE

CRANK CASE

Problem-solving

1 The Stirling engine is a simple hot air engine. Look at the diagram and put the sentences in the correct order to explain how it works.

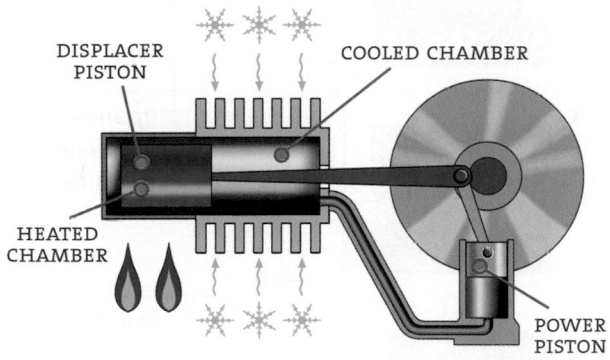

a The air cools and pressure drops in the power cylinder. _____

b This displaces the air to the hot end. _____

c The air heats up rapidly and pushes the power piston back up the cylinder. _____

d This movement rotates the flywheel, drawing the displacer piston to the cold end of the cylinder. _____

e The power piston moves down the cylinder. _____

f When the displacer moves to the hot end of the cylinder, air is displaced to the cold end. _____

g This rotates the flywheel and moves the displacer piston back to the hot end. _____

2 Work in pairs. Decide which factor is the most important to the successful functioning of the engine. Can you explain why?

a The amount of heat applied

b The size of the flywheel

c The type of metal which the piston is made of

d The temperature difference between the ends of the displacer cylinder

e The external air temperature

f The diameter of the displacer cylinder

3 What modern applications can you think of for the Stirling engine?

Pairwork

1 Work in pairs, A and B. Study this photo of an appropriate technology device. Discuss together what it might be.

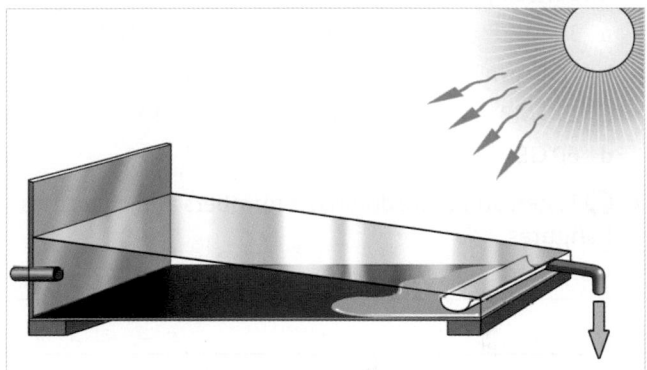

2 Each of you has a diagram of the device. Exchange information with your partner by asking and answering questions. Label all the components.

Student A   Go to p.111.
Student B   Go to p.113.

3 🎧 Together decide how the device operates. Then compare your explanation with the recording

Speaking

1 Study these statements about appropriate technology. Tick (✓) the ones you agree with and cross (✗) those you disagree with.

1 Appropriate technology is only for poor countries. _____

2 Technology students should invent and make appropriate technology devices. _____

3 Studying appropriate technology is a waste of time. _____

4 Appropriate technology is out-of-date technology. _____

2 Now compare your answers with your partner. Discuss the statements you disagree about.

Useful language

Why do you think that…?   *In my opinion, appropriate technology…*

Don't you think that…?   *My view is that…*

plant (n) large industrial machinery
hire (v) let somebody use something for a short time, in return for payment

Pronunciation
Numbers and quantities

1 🎧 Read out the numbers and quantities. Then listen and check your answers.

a 3.142	e 16 kHz	i 12 V DC
b 1150 mm	f 30 mA	j 10^6
c 250 MB	g 0°C	k 10^{-12}
d 60 GB	h 73%	l 40:1

2 🎧 Listen and write down the numbers and quantities in figures.

a _____

b _____

c _____

d _____

e _____

f _____

g _____

h _____

i _____

j _____

» Go to **Symbols and characters** p.114

Vocabulary
Describing motion

1 Match adjectives 1–6 with the diagrams and adverbs A–F.

1 anticlockwise
2 clockwise
3 linear
4 oscillating
5 reciprocating
6 rotary

Movement	Adjective	Adverb
A	_____	–
B	_____	up and down, backwards and forwards
C	_____	in a straight line
D	_____	from side to side
E	_____	clockwise
F	_____	anticlockwise

2 Work in pairs. Take turns to cover each column of the table and test your partner. Tell your partner to draw the arrows and say the vocabulary.

Customer care

Explaining the difference between products

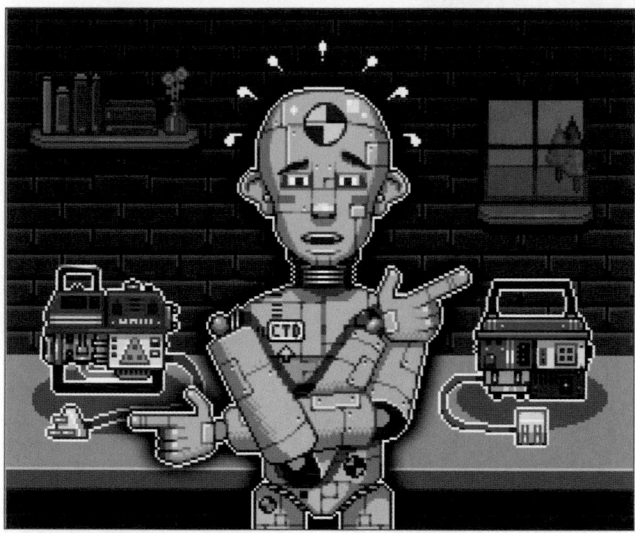

Work in pairs, A and B.

Student A   Go to p.111.

Student B

You are a customer at a **plant** hire company. You want to **hire** a portable generator for two weeks to provide power for your home. You don't want a noisy machine and you only want to fill the tank once a day. It must be easy to use and provide sufficient power for your home. You don't want to pay more than €40 a day.

Useful language
What's the output?
What kind of fuel does it use?
How often do I need to fill it up?
Is it easy to start?
How noisy is it?
How much will it cost?

Key words

Adjectives
rural
sound-proofed
two-stroke

Nouns
accelerator
compression
crankshaft
domestic appliance
exhaust gas
fuel
pulley

Noun and verb
pump

Verbs
charge (batteries)
engage (gears)
generate
wear

Note here anything about how English is used in technology that is **new** to you.

6 Crime-fighting and security

Switch on

Look at the picture of the police officer.
Can you name any of the equipment he carries?

A Item	B Function
torch	provide light, signal

Listening

Crime-fighting equipment

1 🎧 Listen to a police officer talking about his equipment. As you listen, complete column A of the table with all the items he mentions.

2 🎧 Listen again and complete column B of the table with the function of the items.

In this unit
- key terms for crime-fighting and security equipment
- how to describe the function of equipment
- developing the skills of finding and exchanging information
- writing a short report

● Language spot
Describing function

- Study these examples:

*Handcuffs are **used to** restrain someone.*
*The knife-proof vest is **used as** body armour.*
*Radios are **used for** contacting police headquarters.*
*The baton is **for** keeping people at a safe distance.*

- We can describe what things are used for, their function, in these ways:

used to + infinitive
used as + noun
(used) for + -ing

>> Go to **Grammar reference** p.118

1 Match the items in the first column with their function in the second column.

1	tasers	a	help people know exactly where they are
2	Personal Identification Numbers (PINs)	b	incapacitate suspects without serious injury
3	tagging	c	help protect air travellers
4	anti-virus software	d	keep people at a safe distance
5	face-recognition device	e	protect computers
6	helmet	f	admit only the right people
7	batons	g	protect cards from criminal use
8	Global Positioning System (GPS)	h	monitor convicted criminals
9	torches	i	head protection
10	luggage X-ray equipment	j	signalling devices

2 Work in pairs. Take turns to ask and answer questions about the items in **1**.

EXAMPLE

A *What's the function of tagging?*
B *It's used to monitor criminals. What are tasers for?*
A *They're used to incapacitate suspects without serious injury.*

Vocabulary
-proof, -resistant, -tight

1 Study the examples.

a knife-proof vest	*a vest which a knife **can't pass through***
a shock-proof watch	*a watch which **isn't damaged by** shock or **is protected from** shock*
corrosion-resistant steel	*steel which **isn't damaged by** corrosion*
an air-tight seal	*a seal which air **can't pass through***

2 Explain examples 1–8 in the same way.

1 a gas-tight seal
2 weatherproof paint
3 heat-resistant materials
4 a soundproof recording studio
5 rustproof car bodies
6 a foolproof device
7 a water-resistant coat
8 a water-tight container

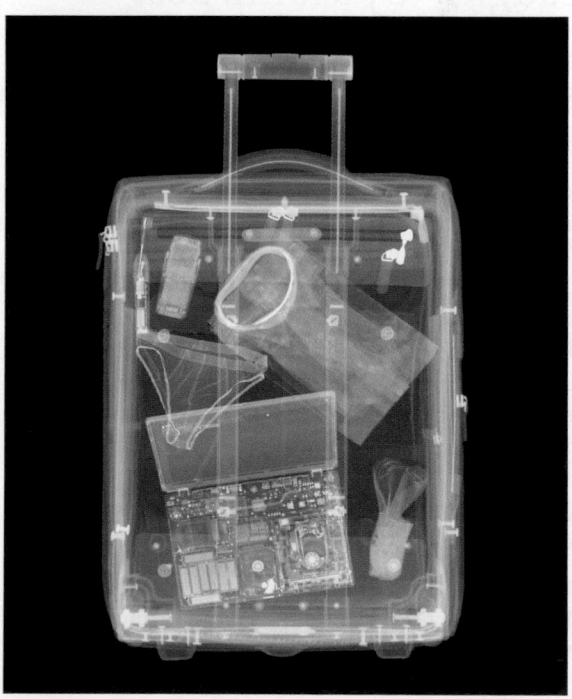

You mustn't smile on your passport photograph as showing your teeth or open mouth can affect face-recognition devices. Also, you mustn't wear glasses with tinted lenses.

Pairwork

1 Work in pairs, A and B. Each of you has a short text about a crime-fighting device. The titles of the texts are:

Student A   Smart gun recognizes its owner

Student B   Caught – by a lamp post

Discuss what you think the texts might be about. Use the pictures opposite to help you.

2 Read your own text. Then find out from your partner this information about his / her device. Ask these questions and make notes of the answers.

1. What is the device called?
2. What does it do?
3. How does it work?
4. Where is it used?
5. How successful is it?

Student A   Go to p.111.

Student B

Caught – by a lamp post

Cities in the UK like London, Glasgow, and Birmingham are fitting a new device to lamp posts in areas which have a crime problem. It's called *Flashcam* and has been developed by an American company, Q Star. It consists of a camera with a motion sensor. If it detects a group of people in an area where there is no reason for them to be, it shouts a warning at them such as: *Stop! If you are engaging in an illegal activity, your photograph will be taken. Please leave the area.* If people don't move, it goes off with a very intense flash and a loud shout. They have had a positive effect in some parts of London in reducing crime and anti-social behaviour.

3 Now read your partner's text and check the information.

4 Discuss what you think are the practical problems of these two devices. Would they work in your country? What modifications would you make?

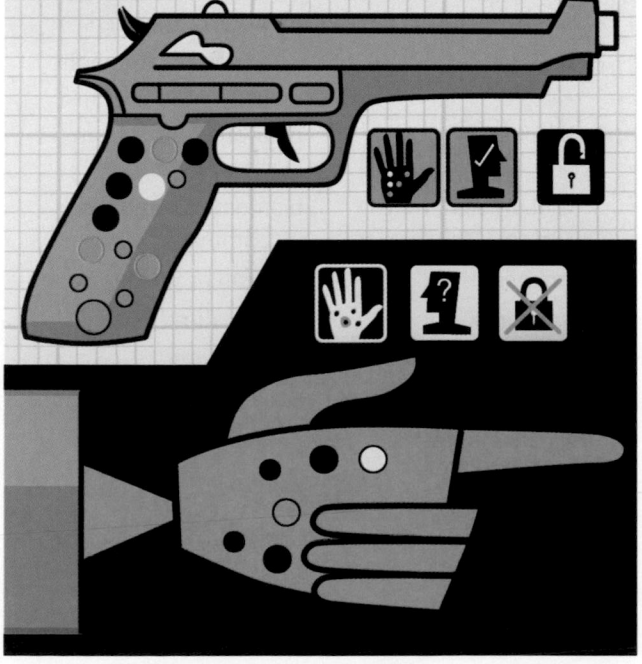

online connections via the Internet
RF connections wireless, by radio frequency signals

Problem-solving

What's the best technical solution to the problem of protecting a large store from *shoplifters* (people who steal things from shops)? Work in small groups and study the solutions, then make your choice. Give reasons for your choice.

CAMERAS

1 CCTV (closed circuit television) cameras with wide-angle lenses.
Signal relayed to a central office and monitored by a security guard.
Recorded on video tapes every day.

Advantages	Disdvantages
• Visible deterrent. Thieves know they may be recorded	• People forget to change tapes
• Not very expensive	• Image may not be very clear
• You can include some dummy cameras	

2 Digital CCTV cameras with **online connections**.
Recorded on hard disk which can store several months of recording.

Advantages	Disdvantages
• Can be viewed from any broadband connection	• Expensive
• No tapes to change	

3 Concealed micro-cameras with **RF connections**.

Advantages	Disdvantages
• No expensive wiring	• Not a visible deterrent
• Good way to catch thieves in action	

TAGS

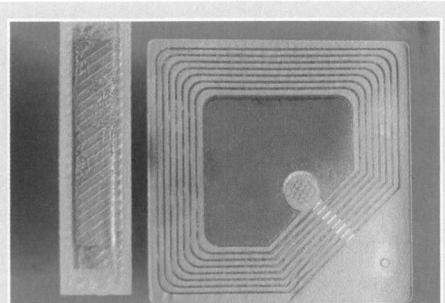

4 Large electronic security tags on things which are often stolen.
Alarm is triggered by an 8.2 MHz signal when the tag is taken through a security gate at the shop entrance.

Advantages	Disdvantages
• Visible deterrent	• Must be removed at tills
• Tags are inexpensive	• Expensive system to install
	• Professional thieves may remove them in the store

5 Concealed electronic security tags.

Advantages	Disdvantages
• Thieves may not see them and so can be caught more easily	• Must be deactivated at tills. Sales people may forget

6 Ink tags on clothing.
They break if wrongly removed and spoil the item.

Advantages	Disdvantages
• Simple and inexpensive deterrent	• Professional thieves can remove them

Gadget box

Rotundus is a spherical robot, invented at the University of Uppsala in Sweden, which can patrol a site or building to guard it. It contains sensors such as cameras, heat and smoke detectors, and microphones. It can send for security forces, sound an alarm, and follow intruders over sand, snow, mud, or water. However, it cannot climb stairs.

Why is *Rotundus* better than a low-tech solution like a security guard or a guard dog?

Writing
Short report and linking words

In writing we often use linking words to make it clear to the reader how the ideas in our writing are connected. We can use *but* to link an advantage and a disadvantage.

EXAMPLE

*Use CCTV cameras and record onto videotapes. This is not very expensive **but** people forget to change the tapes.*

We can also use *however* and *although* to link an advantage and a disadvantage, usually at the start of a sentence.

EXAMPLES

*Use CCTV cameras and record onto videotapes. These cameras are a visible deterrent to thieves. **However**, the image may not be very clear.*
*Use CCTV cameras and record onto videotapes. **Although** these cameras are a visible deterrent to thieves, the image may not be clear.*

We can use *because*, *since*, and *as* to link a recommendation with a reason.

EXAMPLES

*I advise you to install digital CCTV cameras **because** they are effective and not very expensive.*
*I recommend you use large electronic security tags **since** they are a visible deterrent to most thieves.*
*Our advice is to use large electronic security tags **as** they are a visible deterrent to most thieves.*

1 Now write a short report on security for the owner of a large shop. Your report should have two sections:
   1 List the advantages and disadvantages of each solution.
   2 Recommend the best solution. Give reasons to support your choice.

2 Exchange your report from **1** with another student and decide if it can be understood easily. Mark any places where the report is not clear enough.

Customer care
Using informal language

1 Study these three home security systems. Note their advantages and disadvantages.

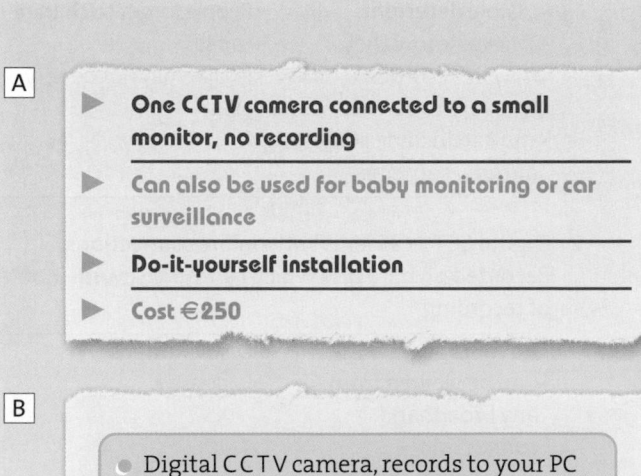

A
  ▶ **One CCTV camera connected to a small monitor, no recording**
  ▶ Can also be used for baby monitoring or car surveillance
  ▶ **Do-it-yourself installation**
  ▶ Cost €250

B
  ● Digital CCTV camera, records to your PC
  ● Fitted with motion sensors which trigger recording when an intruder enters
  ● Professionally installed
  ● Cost €1,000

2 Work with a partner. Take turns to play the roles of Salesperson and Customer.

Salesperson

Use the information in **1** and select from the phrases below to sell the system that best meets the customer's needs. The first row has more formal phrases. The second row has phrases which are more common in informal, spoken English. Choose the language that matches the customer's language.

Customer

Listen to the salesperson and ask questions. Choose the home security system that best meets your needs.

Not satisfactory	Satisfactory	More than satisfactory
it's inadequate	it's adequate	it's ideal / perfect
it falls short / it's not up to the job	it does the job / it fits the bill	it's spot on / it ticks all the boxes

C

Complete home defence system

Wireless, so easy installation

Can be switched on and off with a remote device, so no code numbers have to be remembered and keyed in

Will text you a message when your children get home

Five CCTV cameras activated if an intruder enters your home. System also notifies the security company which advises the police immediately

Will also detect smoke or flooding and notify the emergency services

Cost €3,600 plus a monthly maintenance charge of €30

Checklist

Assess your progress in this unit.
Tick (✓) the statements which are true.

- [ ] I know key terms for crime-fighting and security equipment
- [ ] I can describe the function of security equipment
- [ ] I can write a short report
- [ ] My reading and listening are good enough to understand most of each text in this unit

Key words

Adjectives
low-tech
unique

Nouns
body armour
GPS
grip
motion sensor
PIN
recognition
security
sensor
shock
tagging
trigger

Verbs
escape
incapacitate

Note here anything about how English is used in technology that is **new** to you.

7 Manufacturing

Switch on

1 Manufacturing is about changing materials into products. Choose from the list and complete the table with the materials required for products A–C.

alloy   copper
rubber   plastic
steel   wood
titanium   aluminium

	Materials	Processes
A 		
B 		
C 		

2 Now choose from the list and complete the table with the processes involved in making these products.

assembly   impact extrusion
bending   injection-moulding
bonding   painting
colour printing   plating
cutting   welding

» Go to pp.56–58 for more manufacturing processes

It's my job

1 Work in pairs and answer the questions.

1 What stages are involved in manufacturing bread on a large scale?

2 What kind of technician is responsible for keeping a plant bakery running?

3 What do you think the numbers a–g refer to?

a 225 kg   d 21 minutes   f 10,000

b 3 minutes   e 110 minutes   g 240,000

c 54 minutes

2 🎧 Listen to Nasser Aziz, a Manufacturing Engineer, and check your answers.

3 🎧 Listen again and complete the table to describe what happens at each stage in plant bakery bread-making.

Stage	1	2
What happens	_____ _____	the dough is cut into loaves, put into tins, and left

Stage	3	4
What happens	_____ _____	the loaves are left to cool, then taken out of their tins

Stage	5	6
What happens	_____ _____	_____ _____

Stage	7	
What happens	_____ _____	

● Language spot

Present Passive

● To describe a manufacturing process, we should answer these two important questions about each stage in the process:
What happens?
When does it happen?

● We can answer the *What* question using the Present Passive:
*The ingredients **are mixed**.*

● We can answer the *When* question by numbering the stages (1, 2, 3, etc.), or by using sequence words (*first, then, next, after that, finally*) (see Unit 5):
1 *The ingredients are mixed.*
***First**, the ingredients are mixed.*
***After** the loaves are sliced, they are wrapped.*

● Where necessary, we should also answer these questions:
Where does it happen?
Why does it happen?
How does it happen?

● We can answer the *Where* question by adding information on the place the stage happens:
*The ingredients are mixed **in a steel mixer**.*

● We can answer the *Why* question using the infinitive with *to* (see Unit 6):
*The ingredients are mixed in a steel mixer **to make dough**.*

● We can answer the *How* question like this:
*The loaves are taken out of their tins **(by) using suction**.*

≫ Go to **Grammar reference** p.118

1 Read what Nasser says in the Listening script on p.126. Then complete the *Where*, *Why*, and *How* information in the table with information provided in the text. You do not have all the information for each stage.

Stage	1	2	3
Where	_____	_____	_____
Why	_____		
How			

Stage	4	5	6
Where			_____
Why		_____	
How	_____		_____

Stage	7		
Where			
Why			
How	_____		

2 Now combine the information for each stage into one sentence.

EXAMPLE

1 *First, the ingredients are mixed in a steel mixer to make dough.*

Writing

Short sequence

1 Study the injection moulding machine. It is for manufacturing plastic products like CD cases. Then put the stages in the injection moulding process in the correct sequence. The first and last stages are done for you.

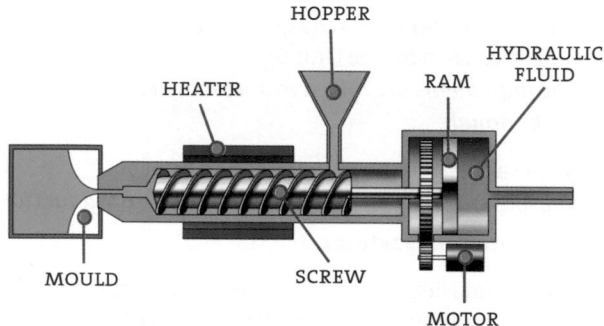

HOPPER

HEATER

RAM

HYDRAULIC FLUID

MOULD

SCREW

MOTOR

1   The hopper is filled with plastic.

a   The plastic is carried through the barrel by the rotating screw.

b   The hot plastic is injected quickly into the mould.

c   The plastic is melted by the heaters.

d   The plastic travels through the barrel.

e   The plastic is fed into the barrel.

f   There is enough melted plastic in the barrel.

g   The mould is cool.

h   The plastic is left to set before the pressure is removed.

i   The screw is pushed forward by the ram.

11   The finished moulding is removed.

2 Combine the pairs of sentences using suitable time words (see Unit 5).

1   d + c   2   f + i   3   g + 11

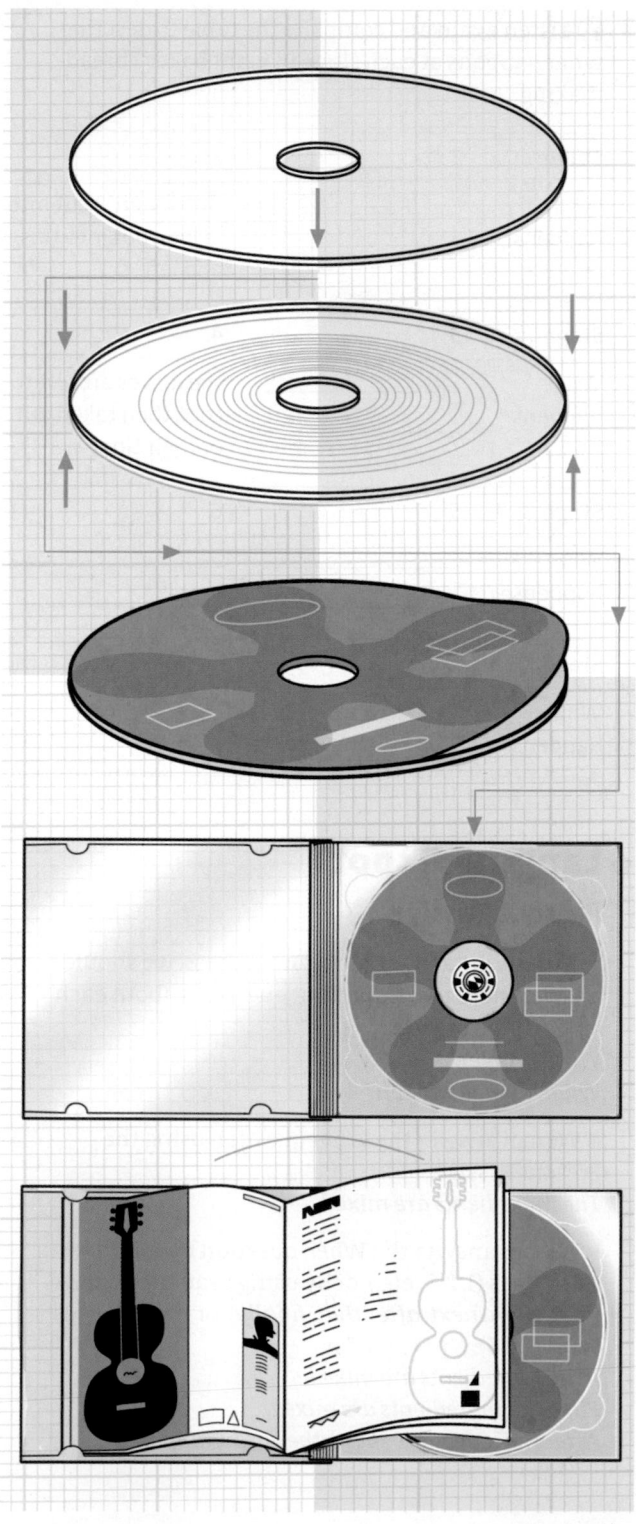

Pairwork

1 Work in pairs, A and B. Study this diagram of the stages in the manufacture of CDs. With the help of the diagram, discuss how CDs are made.

2 Each of you has a set of short texts describing some of the stages. Try to match each of your texts to one of the stages in the diagram. Be careful – some of the stages are not shown in the diagram.

3 Discuss your information with your partner and agree on the correct order for all of the texts.

Student A   Go to p.111.
Student B

D   From the Father, multiple positive image metal Mothers are made by electroforming. Each Mother in turn produces a negative image Son which is also known as a stamper.

E   The glass master disc is placed in a chemical bath. The resist coating is not affected but where the laser has removed the resist, the chemical etches tiny pits into the surface of the glass.

F   Each disc is finished by applying a thin coating of aluminium to form a reflective layer. The disc is then covered with a protective coating of clear plastic, inspected, and labelled.

Speaking

1 Work in groups of three. Make a list of at least nine food and drink products which, like bread, are manufactured on a large scale.

2 Choose one from your list and try to explain to the others in your group how it is made using your own knowledge of the process.

3 Now combine information as a group to try to make a better explanation. Using any useful information your partners have provided, repeat the explanation.

4 The next person should now choose a topic. Continue until everyone has given three explanations.

Useful language
I think ... happens next.
You've forgotten about ...
What about ... ?

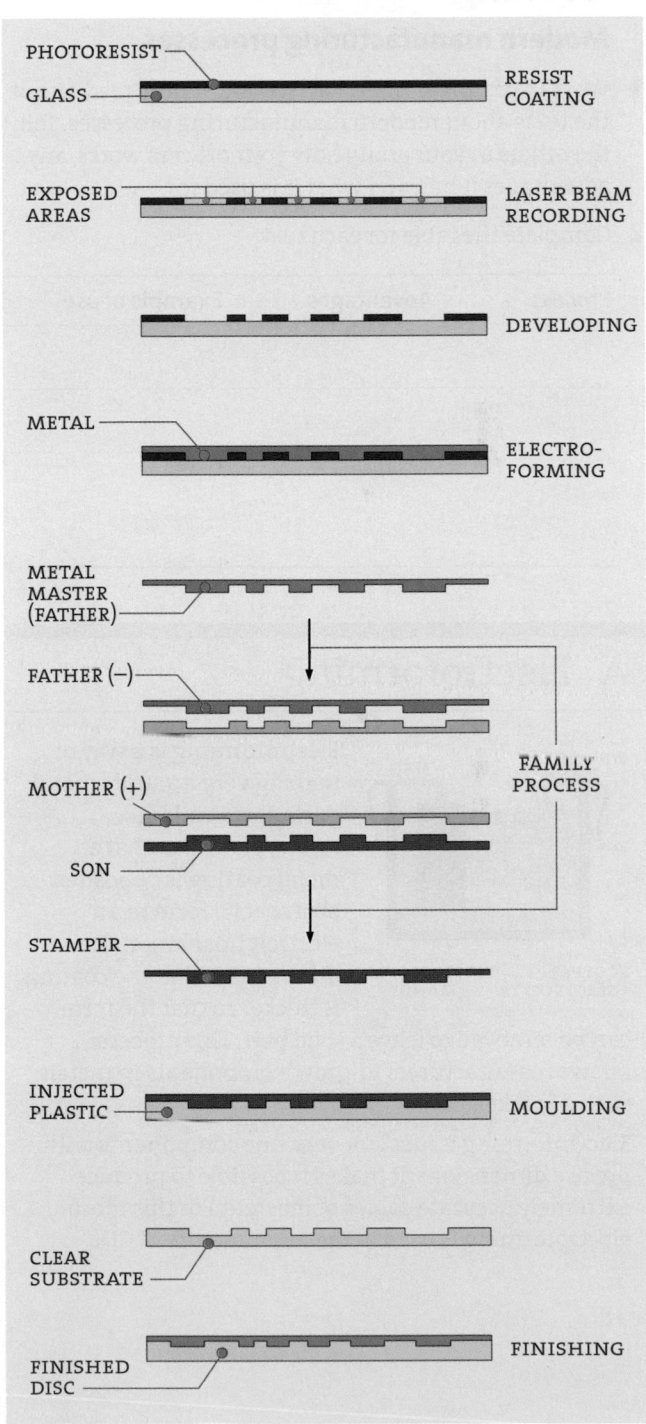

PHOTORESIST
GLASS
RESIST COATING

EXPOSED AREAS
LASER BEAM RECORDING

DEVELOPING

METAL
ELECTRO-FORMING

METAL MASTER (FATHER)

FATHER (−)

MOTHER (+)

SON

FAMILY PROCESS

STAMPER

INJECTED PLASTIC
MOULDING

CLEAR SUBSTRATE

FINISHED DISC
FINISHING

Reading

Modern manufacturing processes

1 Work in groups of three. Each of you should read **one** of the texts about modern manufacturing processes. Tell the others in your group how your process works, any advantages it has, and what it is used for.

2 Complete the table for each text.

Process	Advantages	Example of use

A Electroforming

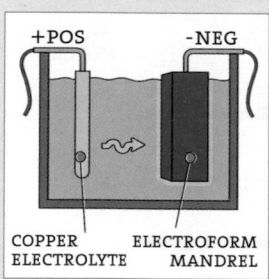

Electroforming is a way of making very accurate metal parts. It is similar to electroplating in that a metal coating is deposited on a special form in an electrolytic solution. The difference is that the coating is thicker so that the form can be removed to leave a solid part. This process allows manufacturers to 'grow' components in metals such as nickel.

Electroforming is ideal for very fine components with precise dimensions. It makes it possible to produce extremely accurate copies of masters. For this reason, electroforming is used in the manufacture of CDs.

B Water jet abrasive cutting

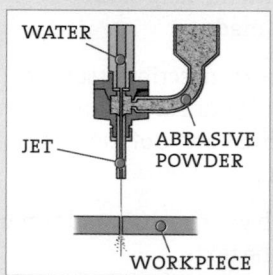

Water jet abrasive cutting uses a high pressure jet of water combined with an abrasive substance to cut through materials. The advantages of this form of cutting are that the jet can be adjusted and the kind of abrasive changed so that almost any kind of material can be cut. In addition, the material can be cut without changing its properties in any way. With heat, there is always some damage to the areas nearest the cut.

This form of cutting has many applications. It can be used to cut metals, composites, and even thick concrete. At the other end of the scale, fine water jets, without added abrasives, are used in surgery.

C Hydroforming

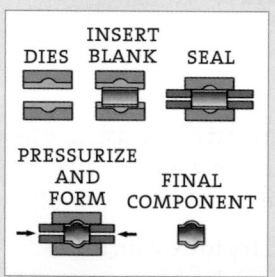

Hydroforming is a way of shaping materials such as aluminium or ultralight steel. The metal is pushed into shape using fluid pressure. For example, to produce components for car bodies, steel tubes are placed inside a mould and high pressure applied in the tube which pushes the metal into the exact shape required. Hydroforming a component in this way means that several different operations such as stamping and welding are no longer required.

Hydroforming is used where there is demand for lower weight with high strength. It is used in the manufacture of top-of-the-range sports cars and motorbikes, such as Harley Davidsons. It is also used in the aerospace industry to produce panels for aircraft.

Vocabulary

Compound nouns

Compounds nouns are often used in technical English. They consist of two nouns working together. Study these examples.

car bodies = **bodies** of **cars**
plastic baths = **baths** made of **plastic**
injection moulding = **moulding** by **injection**
gas oven = **oven** which uses **gas**
gas canister = **canister** for **gas**

Explain compound nouns 1–8 in the same way.

1 computer covers _____
2 vacuum forming _____
3 pvc pipes _____
4 plane wings _____
5 steel mixer _____
6 wind pump _____
7 steel bearings _____
8 clockwork radio _____

Webquest

Use a search engine such as Google to find out what processes are used in the manufacture of items 1–5 and complete the table. (Tip: do an exact phrase search like this: "car bodies are made by")

Item	Process
1 car bodies	
2 computer case	
3 plane wings	
4 plastic baths	
5 pvc pipes	

Key words

Nouns
barrel
blade
bonding
extrusion
hopper
ingredients
plant
plating
process
ram
saw
suction
welding

Verbs
cool
spray

Note here anything about how English is used in technology that is **new** to you.

8 Transport

Switch on

1 Identify the different forms of transport in pictures A–F.

2 Work in small groups. List other types of land, sea, and air transport.

A

B

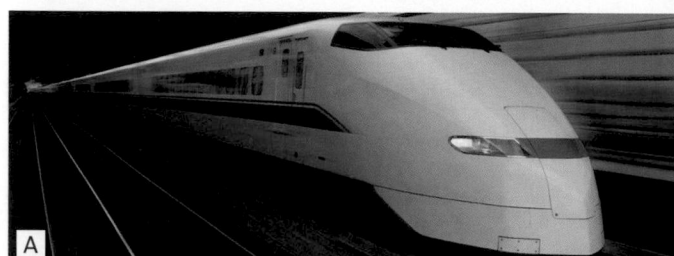

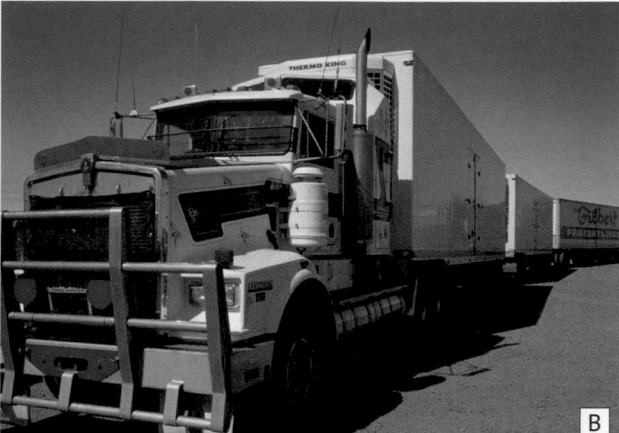

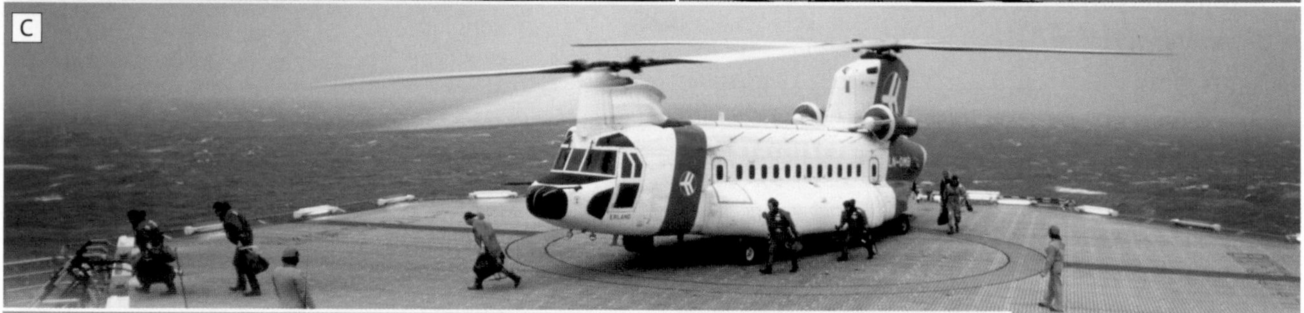

C

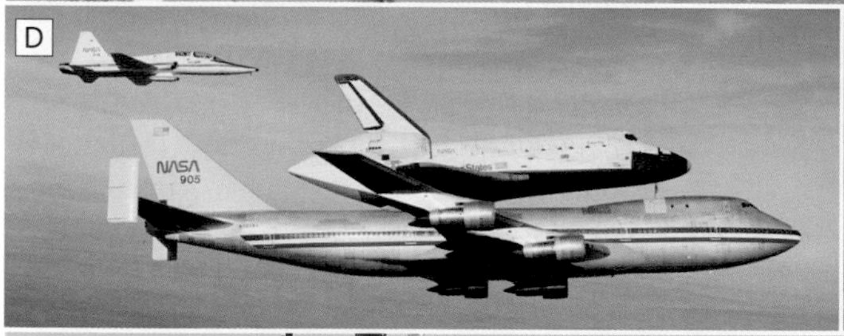

D

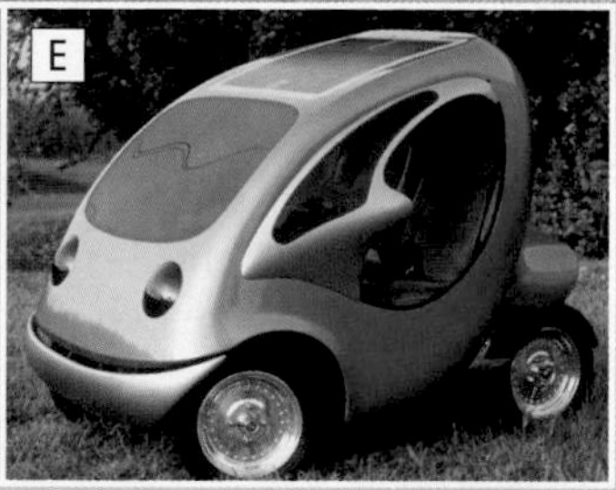

E

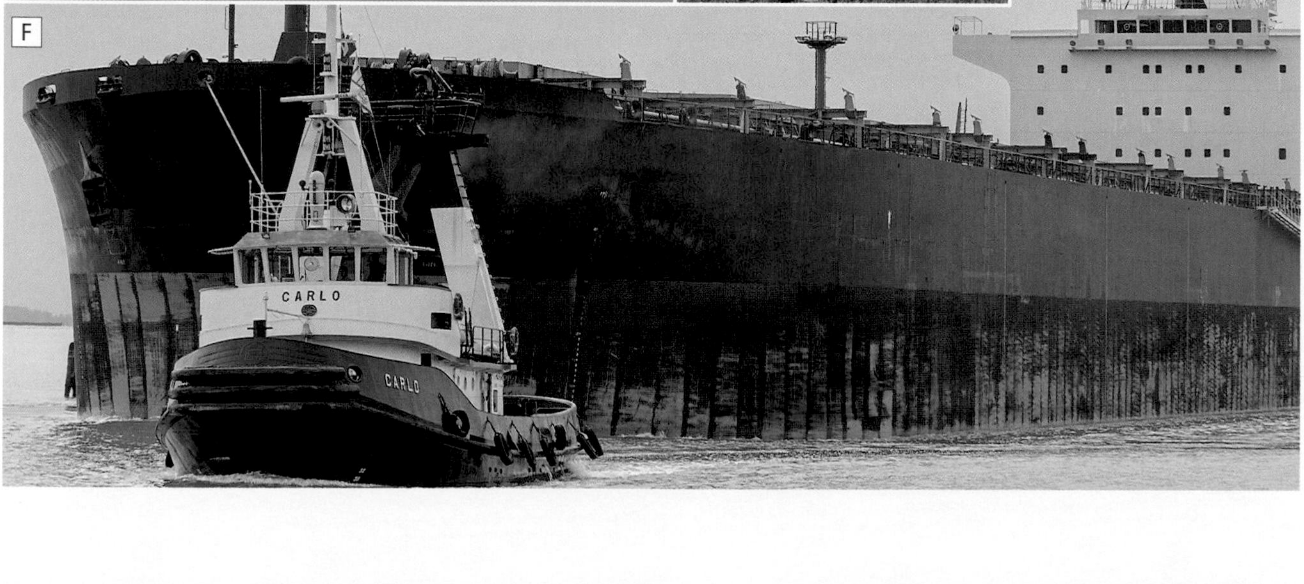

F

In this unit
- key terms for different forms of transport
- how to make predictions using *will, may, might*
- how to use corrective stress
- reading and listening for detail
- using your search skills to find out more about cars of the future

Reading
The car of the future

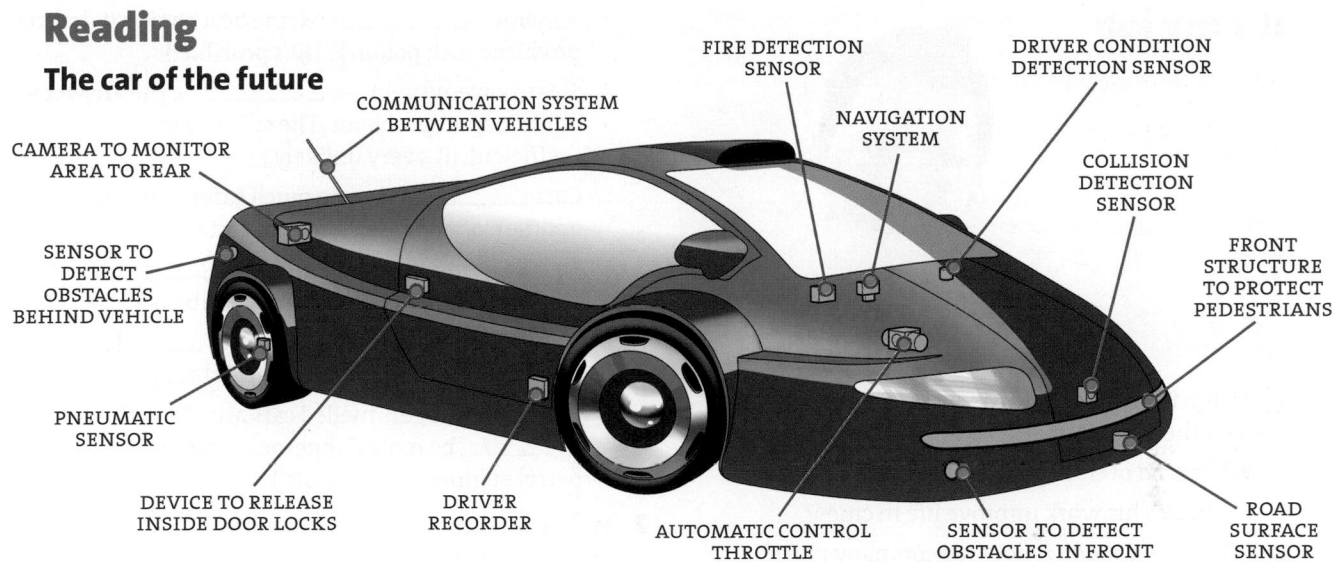

COMMUNICATION SYSTEM BETWEEN VEHICLES

FIRE DETECTION SENSOR

DRIVER CONDITION DETECTION SENSOR

NAVIGATION SYSTEM

CAMERA TO MONITOR AREA TO REAR

COLLISION DETECTION SENSOR

SENSOR TO DETECT OBSTACLES BEHIND VEHICLE

FRONT STRUCTURE TO PROTECT PEDESTRIANS

PNEUMATIC SENSOR

DEVICE TO RELEASE INSIDE DOOR LOCKS

DRIVER RECORDER

AUTOMATIC CONTROL THROTTLE

SENSOR TO DETECT OBSTACLES IN FRONT

ROAD SURFACE SENSOR

1 Look at the diagram and answer the questions.

1 How is this car different from a typical car of today?

2 What do you think ASV means?

3 What are the aims of the designers of this car?

4 What further improvements could you make to this car?

2 Read the text and check your answers to questions 1–3 in **1**.

3 Read the last paragraph of the text again and note the advantages and disadvantages of the forms of power in the table.

	Advantages	Disadvantages
1 electric		
2 hybrid (petrol and electric)		
3 LPG		
4 hydrogen fuel cell		

ASVs

Road traffic is increasing worldwide. This increase brings problems: road accidents, congestion, and pollution. However, engineers are working on Advanced safety vehicles (ASVs) which will be much safer for drivers, other road users such as cyclists, and for pedestrians. They are also working on new engines which use cleaner fuels.

ASVs will be equipped with electronic sensors to prevent accidents and to make it safer for people when accidents do happen. One sensor will stop the driver falling asleep. Others will warn drivers when they are too close to other vehicles.

The car of the future might be electric. Electric motors are very efficient and produce no pollution, but they need heavy batteries and their range is limited with current technology. Hybrid cars have both a petrol engine and an electric motor. They save about 15% of fuel. They need batteries but they don't have to be charged overnight as the motor acts as a generator when the car brakes. Liquefied petroleum gas (LPG) is already used as a fuel. Cars can be converted easily but LPG only cuts down pollution a little. Hydrogen fuel cells may be the long-term answer. They provide clean power but each cell is very expensive.

Gadget box

ENV is the world's first hydrogen-powered motorbike and can reach 80 kph in 12 seconds. It produces no pollution and is almost silent. However, the hydrogen fuel cell is expensive and some motorbike fans don't like the idea of a 'noise-free' bike! How could you make this motorbike more attractive to bikers?

It's my job

1 🎧 Listen to Jan Bronec, a Mechanical Engineer, and answer the questions.

1 What kind of transport is he concerned with?

2 How does his work improve life in cities?

3 What other product does his company make?

4 What kind of fuel does this product use?

5 Why might he have more opportunity to use English?

● Language spot

Prediction: *will, may, might*

● Study these examples:
Advanced safety vehicles (ASVs) **will** *be much safer.*
The car of the future **might** *be electric.*
Hydrogen fuel cells **may** *be the long-term answer.*

When we are talking about future developments, we use *will* for things which are certain. We use *may* and *might* for things which are possible. (There is little difference between *may* and *might* in written English.)

Note these short forms used in spoken English:
won't = will not
mightn't = might not

NOT ~~mayn't~~

≫ Go to **Grammar reference** p.119

1 Complete the sentences using *will, may / might*, or their negative forms. The phrases in brackets will help.

1 We _____ use petrol engines in the future. There are better alternatives. (I'm certain.)

2 Hydrogen fuel cells _____ get cheaper as technology improves. (I'm certain.)

3 A hybrid car _____ be the best choice. It doesn't produce much pollution. (It's possible.)

4 Solar-powered vehicles _____ be the answer to our transport problems. The cells are very inefficient. (It's very unlikely.)

5 Cars _____ become much safer with the addition of many sensors. (I'm certain.)

6 By 2015 more people in Europe _____ travel to work by train than by car. (It's possible.)

7 As world oil supplies dry up, petrol _____ get more and more expensive. (I'm certain.)

8 Because hydrogen-fuelled cars are silent, they _____ be more dangerous than cars with petrol engines. (It's possible.)

2 Make your own predictions about the topics below for ten years into the future. Then compare your predictions with your partner. Try to reach agreement.

● the number of cars in your country

● the price of oil

● the size of passenger aircraft

● the most popular way to travel to work

● the use of electric cars

Pronunciation

Corrective stress

When we correct what someone says, we often stress the point of disagreement.

1 🎧 Listen to this example.

A *Electric motors aren't very efficient.*

B *No, electric motors **are** very efficient.*

2 Correct statements 1–8. Use the words in brackets where provided.

1 Hybrid cars have a diesel engine and an electric motor. (petrol)

2 Hydrogen fuel cells are cheap.

3 Most car drivers are happy to use public transport.

4 LPG cuts down pollution a lot. (little)

5 ASVs are more dangerous for pedestrians. (safer)

6 Solar power is the answer to our transport problems.

7 Air travel is good for the environment.

8 Trains and cars are examples of public transport. (buses)

3 Work in pairs. Take turns to correct each other using the statements above.

4 🎧 Listen and check your answers.

5 Work in pairs. Make statements of your own about the topics below. Disagree with your partner's views and give reasons to support your case. Use the dialogues in **4** as a model.

- the best car made in Europe
- the safest way to travel
- travelling by air
- studying English
- travel by train in the past and now
- the best motorbike
- the answer to traffic problems
- the most interesting job in technology

Problem-solving

1 Work in pairs. Can you identify the less common forms of transport in pictures A–E? Decide who might use them and for what purpose.

2 In your pairs, decide what special features these forms of transport require to operate effectively.

328.767 mph / 529.33 kph
JCB breaks the land-speed record for a diesel
engine vehicle (August 2006)

Customer care
Making and acknowledging apologies

If your company supplies faulty goods or if there is a
delay in providing a service or meeting an order, you
may have to apologize to the customer.

We can apologize face-to-face, by phone, or by email
using phrases like these:

*I'm sorry that your order is late. We've been very busy
but I'll see to it at once.*
Sorry about the delay with your order.

We can acknowledge the apology using phrases like
these:
That's all right. / OK.   *It's not a problem.*
Don't worry about it.   *No problem.*

Sometimes we want to acknowledge the apology
and make sure that action is taken. In this case we add
but ... .

EXAMPLE
*It's not a problem but I'd like them to arrive tomorrow at
the latest.*

Work in pairs. Take turns making and acknowledging
apologies for the problems below. The customer starts
by explaining the problem.

- The car batteries you received are for an old model –
  you wanted the ones for the new model.

- You are still waiting for an important delivery of
  solar panels, due this morning.

- One of the office telephones you received yesterday
  is faulty.

Vocabulary
Recording new expressions

In Unit 1 you studied useful ways of recording new
vocabulary by grouping words according to **subjects**. It
is also useful to group expressions by **function** – what
they are used for.

1 Study the expressions for apologizing in the table of
functions.

Function	Expression
Apologizing	*I'm sorry that ...* *Sorry about ...* *I / We apologize for ...* *I / We regret ...*
Opening a letter or email	
Closing a letter or email	
Referring to previous contact	
Giving reasons	
Promising action	

2 Now complete the table with the expressions below
used for writing emails.

- a   Hi ...
- b   We will ...
- c   I'm writing to you because ...
- d   Regards ...
- e   Dear ...
- f   I wrote to you on (date) ...
- g   We're going to ...
- h   We spoke (last week) ...
- i   Best wishes ...
- j   The reason I'm getting in touch is ...
- k   I can assure you that ...

3 Write a short email to a customer apologizing for
sending five air-conditioning units instead of the six he
/ she ordered. In your email, you should refer to the
telephone conversation you had yesterday and provide
a reason for the error and tell him / her you will send
the remaining unit by express delivery.

Webquest

Search the sites for details of cars which do not have
conventional petrol or diesel engines. Copy the details
into this table for each model.

Make	Model	Price	Engine type	CO_2 emissions

- www.bmw.com
- www.daihatsu.com
- www.ford.com
- www.gm.com
- www.automobiles.honda.com
- www.mercedes-benz.com
- www.smart.com
- www.suzuki.com
- www.toyota.com
- www.volvo.com

Key words

Adjectives
automatic
efficient
hybrid
liquefied
pneumatic

Nouns
congestion
delay
fuel cell
production
public transport
throttle

Verbs
convert
detect
give up
monitor

Note here anything about how English is used
in technology that is **new** to you.

Reading bank

Technology in sport

1 How can clothing help athletes to perform better?

2 Scan the text quickly to find out which items of sportswear are:
   a designed for swimmers
   b designed for runners
   c designed by Adidas
   d designed to reduce drag.

3 Now read the text again to find the answers to these questions.

   1 How does the Precool vest improve performance?

   2 Why did the designers of Fastskin work with an expert in sharks?

   3 What are Power socks designed to prevent and why is this important?

   4 In addition to reducing drag, how does Swift suit help athletes?

   5 How are Strapless goggles held on the swimmer's face?

File Edit View Insert Format Tools Actions Help

High-tech sportswear

Sports companies are always trying to develop new sportswear that will allow athletes to perform more efficiently. Recent developments include:

PRECOOL VEST
Nike has developed a vest which holds ice packs in its lining. It is designed for athletes who compete in marathons and other long distance races. Wearing it for one hour before the race will reduce the body temperature by 19%, and therefore reduces the risk of heat injury.

FASTSKIN

Speedo has designed a swimsuit which it claims is the world's fastest. The designers have worked with an expert on sharks – famously fast swimmers of the fish world. The material copies features of sharkskin and is designed to reduce drag. The makers say it can increase performance by up to 4%.

POWER SOCKS
Adidas produces knee-length socks for runners which are designed to reduce leg fatigue. The socks save energy by compressing the muscles in the legs. This prevents the muscles vibrating each time the runner's foot hits the ground. The vibration is a waste of energy.

SWIFT SUIT
Adidas has designed an aerodynamic head-to-ankle suit for sprinters, cyclists, rowers, and ice-skaters. It keeps athletes cool and reduces drag. The designer claims it gives a ten-centimetre advantage in a 100-metre sprint.

STRAPLESS GOGGLES
For swimmers, Nike has developed featherweight carbon goggles without straps. Each lens is stuck to the eye socket with medical glue. Having no straps, the goggles produce less drag than ordinary goggles.

Appropriate technology

1 Study the diagram of this mechanical device. Choose its correct function.

a   farming

b   exploding mines

c   travelling on the Moon

d   filming in dangerous places

e   carrying things

2 List some of the components of this device in the table.

3 Now read the description of how the device works to find the answer to these questions.

1   What is the device called?

2   What does it do?

3   Why is it suitable for the developing world?

4   Why do the wheels have steel teeth?

5   How often does a wheel have to be changed?

6   Why does the machine not miss any mine in its path?

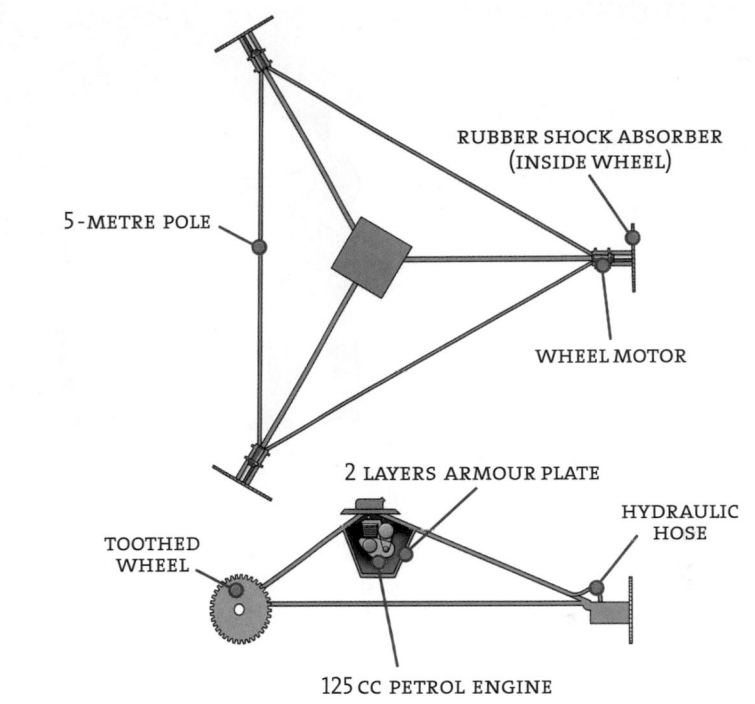

Item	Quantity
5-metre metal or bamboo poles	3

Three-wheeled life-saver

The device is called a Dervish. It is a mine-detonating vehicle for clearing anti-personnel mines from farmland in developing world countries. It has a very simple design and uses inexpensive parts. The United Nations estimates that 24,000 people die each year because of mines.

The Dervish has three wheels. Each wheel has steel teeth to create more pressure. When the teeth pass over a mine, it explodes. The wheels can explode around 1,500 mines before they have to be changed.

A motorbike engine powers the Dervish. The device rotates. As each wheel passes a certain point in the rotation, it slows down. This makes the machine advance in tight circles, about 30 mm apart. For this reason no mine in its path is missed.

Crime-fighting and security

1 Read one of these texts, A, B, or C, as your teacher directs. Find out the answers to these questions.

   1 What is this device or system called?

   2 Who uses it?

   3 How does it work?

2 Share your answers with others in your group.

3 Read the other two texts and see if you can find any extra information.

A Shock tactics

The Advanced taser gun is an electric stun gun which allows police to deal with violent people without causing injury or death. It has a laser sight to make sure the suspect is properly targeted. It uses a compressed air cartridge to fire two darts at the suspect. The darts pull behind them fine electric cable. They can penetrate the thickest clothing, up to 5 centimetres, at a range of 6.4 metres.

When the darts hit someone, the gun delivers a 50,000 volt shock for five seconds. The shock causes temporary paralysis. Taser waves, electrical signals, cause the suspect's muscles to contract. The guns contain a microchip which records the date and time of each firing.

B Eyes don't lie

The iris is the coloured ring round the central part of your eye. Each one is different, which makes it perfect for security systems such as Iris-scanning.

First, your iris is scanned and the information converted to a digital file which is stored in a database. This process takes about three minutes. When you go to a high-security area, you simply look at a camera which scans your iris. The result is compared with your database entry. It takes just over a second to complete the check.

The system is used at airports to speed passengers through passport control and to control entry to restricted areas. Some banks use it at ATM machines instead of PINs.

Apart from the speed, the advantage is that users don't need to remember a password or key. The system can handle users wearing glasses, contact lenses, and also changes to the eye as people age. So far, it's foolproof.

Offender tracking consists of a small tracking unit worn on the belt or ankle. It uses the technology of Global positioning system (GPS) to record the wearer's movements. This data is fed to a server which matches movements with places. Some offenders are restricted to an area around their home. If they move outside that area, this is reported by email to the police. Some offenders are forbidden to enter certain areas. If they go there, this is reported automatically to the police. The system also contains details of crimes. If an offender is near the scene of a crime at the right time, a report is sent directly to the police.

C GPS helps track offenders

Manufacturing

Study the diagrams of common manufacturing processes on pp.56–58.

From the list below, identify the process and method involved in each of these operations.

1 Making a small circular hole in a metal sheet.

2 Joining two similar metals using heat.

3 Applying a permanent layer of chromium to a steel car body part.

4 Gluing wings to the body of an aircraft.

5 Making aluminium components by pouring hot metal into a shaped container.

6 Making plastic bottles by blowing air into a hot plastic tube.

7 Forcing aluminium through a die to make window frames.

8 Shaping steel by hammering an ingot of hot metal.

9 Spraying a component with tiny particles of resin and colour to make a protective and attractive covering.

10 Cutting a metal sheet into two using a sharp blade.

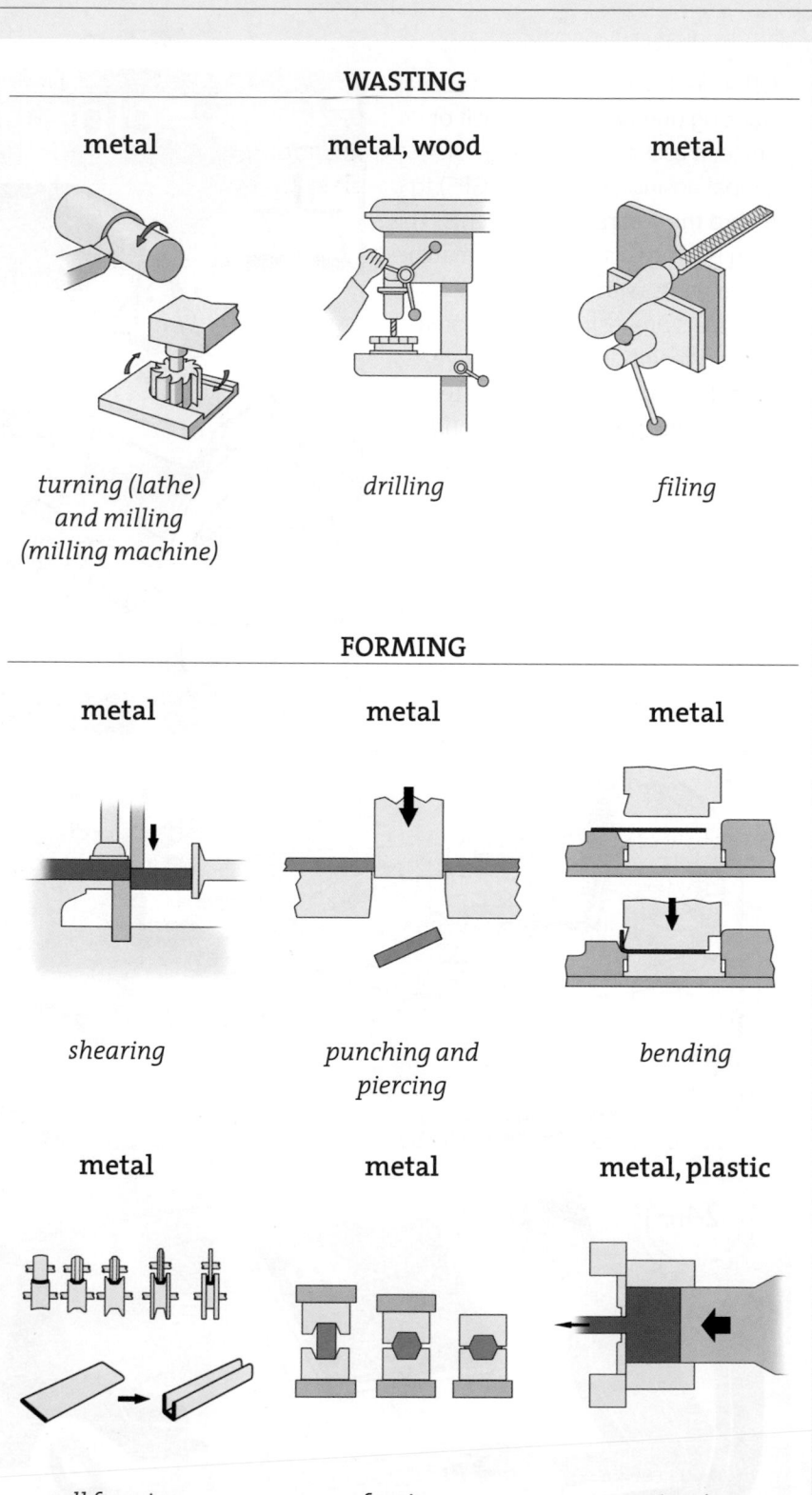

WASTING

metal — turning (lathe) and milling (milling machine)

metal, wood — drilling

metal — filing

FORMING

metal — shearing

metal — punching and piercing

metal — bending

metal — roll forming

metal — forging

metal, plastic — extrusion

CASTING AND MOULDING

metal	metal, polymers, and plastic	plastic	plastic

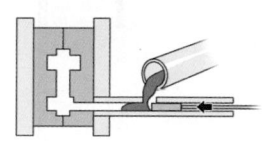
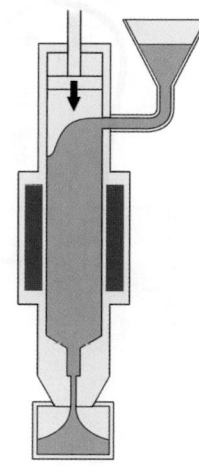
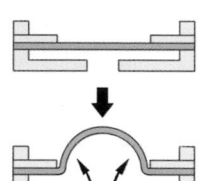
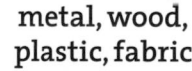
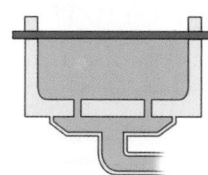
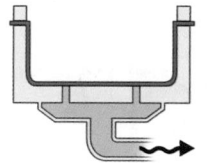
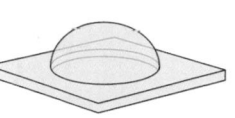
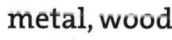

sand casting and die casting	*injection moulding*	*blow moulding*	*vacuum forming*

JOINING AND ASSEMBLY

metal	metal	metal, wood, plastic, fabric	metal, wood

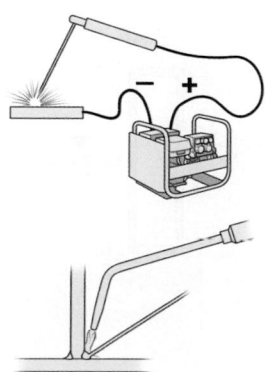
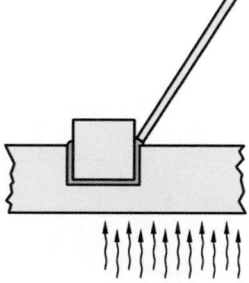
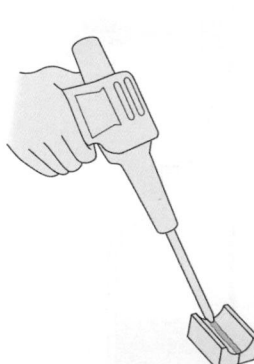
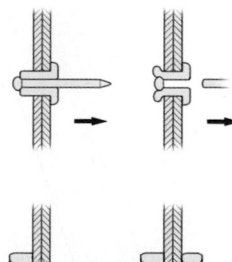
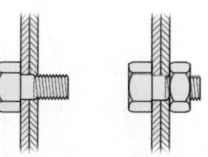

arc welding and gas welding	*brazing*	*using adhesives*	*using mechanical fixings (rivets, screws, bolts, etc.)*

CLEANING AND COATING

metal

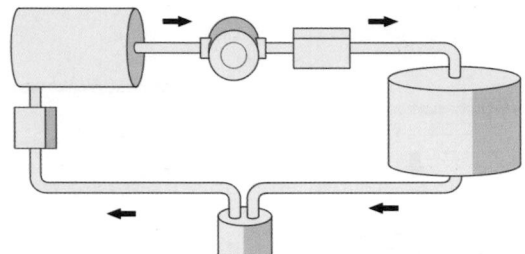

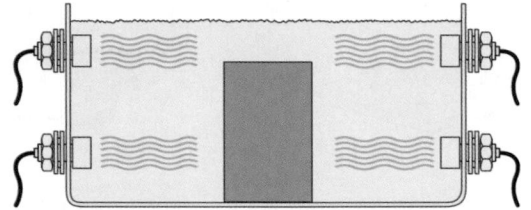

chemical cleaning and ultrasonic cleaning

metal

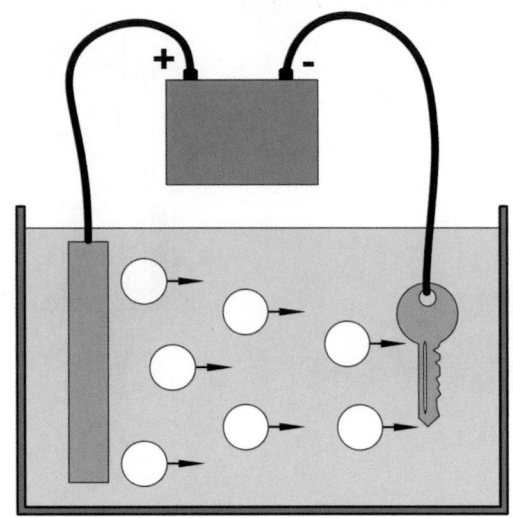

plating

metal, wood, plastic

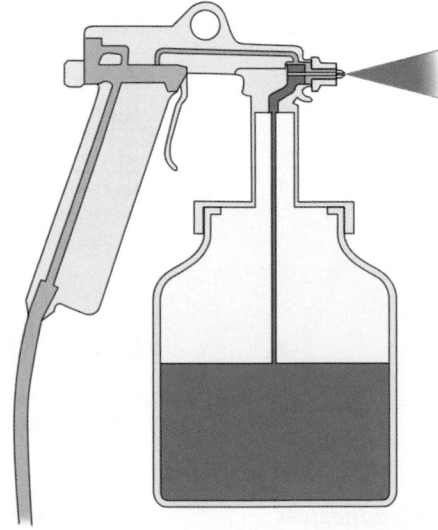

painting

metal

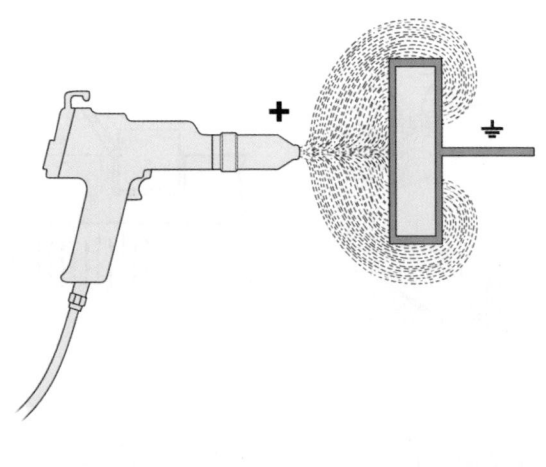

powder coating

Transport

1 A hybrid results from combining two different things. What two things are combined to make a hybrid car? Look at the diagram and check your answer.

2 Read the text and find the answers to these questions.

1 When is the petrol engine used alone?

2 When is the electric motor used alone?

3 When are both motors used?

4 What advantage does this car have over an electric car?

5 How is the battery charged?

Hybrid cars

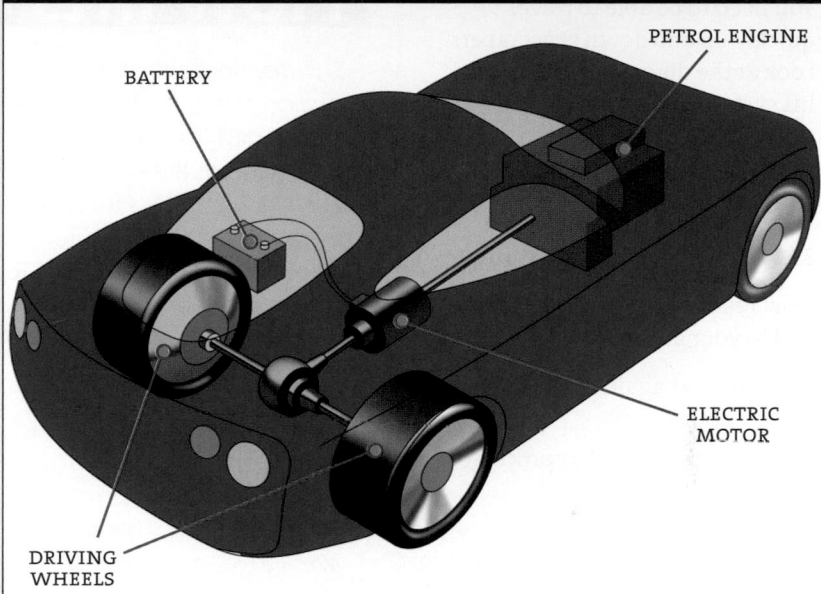

BATTERY

PETROL ENGINE

ELECTRIC MOTOR

DRIVING WHEELS

A Hybrid-electric vehicle (HEV) has both a petrol engine and an electric motor. The petrol engine is the main power source. It is smaller and lighter than the engines of conventional cars. The electric motor provides extra power when needed. In some HEVs, it is connected to the wheels by the same transmission. In addition to a fuel tank, the HEV carries a pack of advanced batteries. There is also a processor which decides when to use the motor and engine.

When the car is running at a constant speed, cruising, the petrol engine provides all the power required. For overtaking, hill climbing, and accelerating from stop, the electric motor provides extra power. In some cars, the motor also provides power for low-speed cruising as petrol engines are least efficient in these conditions.

HEVs use regenerative braking. When the driver brakes, the resistance of the motor helps to slow down the car. At the same time, the energy from the wheels turns the motor which then functions as a generator, producing electricity to recharge the batteries. When the batteries are low, the petrol engine also drives the generator.

HEVs have automatic start / shutoff. The petrol engine shuts off when the car comes to a stop. When the driver presses the accelerator, the motor instantly starts the engine again. No energy is wasted from idling when the car is stopped.

HEVs are more efficient and pollute less than cars with only petrol engines. They do not require special fuel like hydrogen cars and, unlike electric cars, they do not need to be plugged in overnight to recharge the batteries. However, they are heavy because of the weight of the batteries.

High living: skyscrapers

1 You need to be able to travel quickly up and down skyscrapers. Look at the diagram opposite of a lift system and answer these questions.

   1 What is the counterweight for?

   2 What are the guide rails for?

   3 What are the safety features?

2 Now read the text to check and to add to your answers.

3 Read the text again and answer the questions.

   1 What does the microprocessor do?

   2 Why is travel in lifts one of the safest journeys you can make?

How lifts work

The development of tall buildings and lifts go together. The first lifts, or 'elevators' in American English, consisted of a platform suspended from a rope which passed over a pulley at the top of the building. If the rope broke, the platform fell to the ground. In 1852 Elisha Otis invented the first safety lift. If the rope broke, a brake was applied automatically which locked the platform in place between guide rails. Today the Otis company is the largest supplier of lifts in the world.

Most lifts today are roped lifts. The car runs between vertical guide rails which keep it steady and act as a safety device. Steel ropes, or cables, attached to the roof of the car pass over a pulley, called the drive sheave, which is turned by an electric motor. The other end of the cable is attached to a counterweight. This matches the weight of a car with an average load of passengers.

The counterweight saves energy. Its weight helps to raise the car. In the same way, the weight of the car when it descends helps to raise the counterweight. For the most part, the motor only has to overcome friction.

Lifts are controlled by a microprocessor in the machine room. This logs all passenger calls and monitors the number of passengers travelling from floor to floor, the position of any car in the system, and its speed. It can direct passengers to the car which will get them to their destination fastest and will prevent any car which is overloaded from moving.

Lifts have many safety devices which make it virtually impossible for an accident to happen. The cables consist of up to eight steel ropes wound together. Each one is strong enough to support the car. If the car starts to run too quickly, a 'governor', or safety brake, locks the car to the guide rails. Doors on each floor ensure that no one can fall down an open lift shaft. Doors on the car ensure that no passenger can be injured by contact with the shaft. The car cannot move until both sets of doors are closed. Finally, at the bottom of the shaft there are large shock absorbers, or buffers, to cushion the impact of any fall. All these things combined make travel in lifts one of the safest journeys you can make!

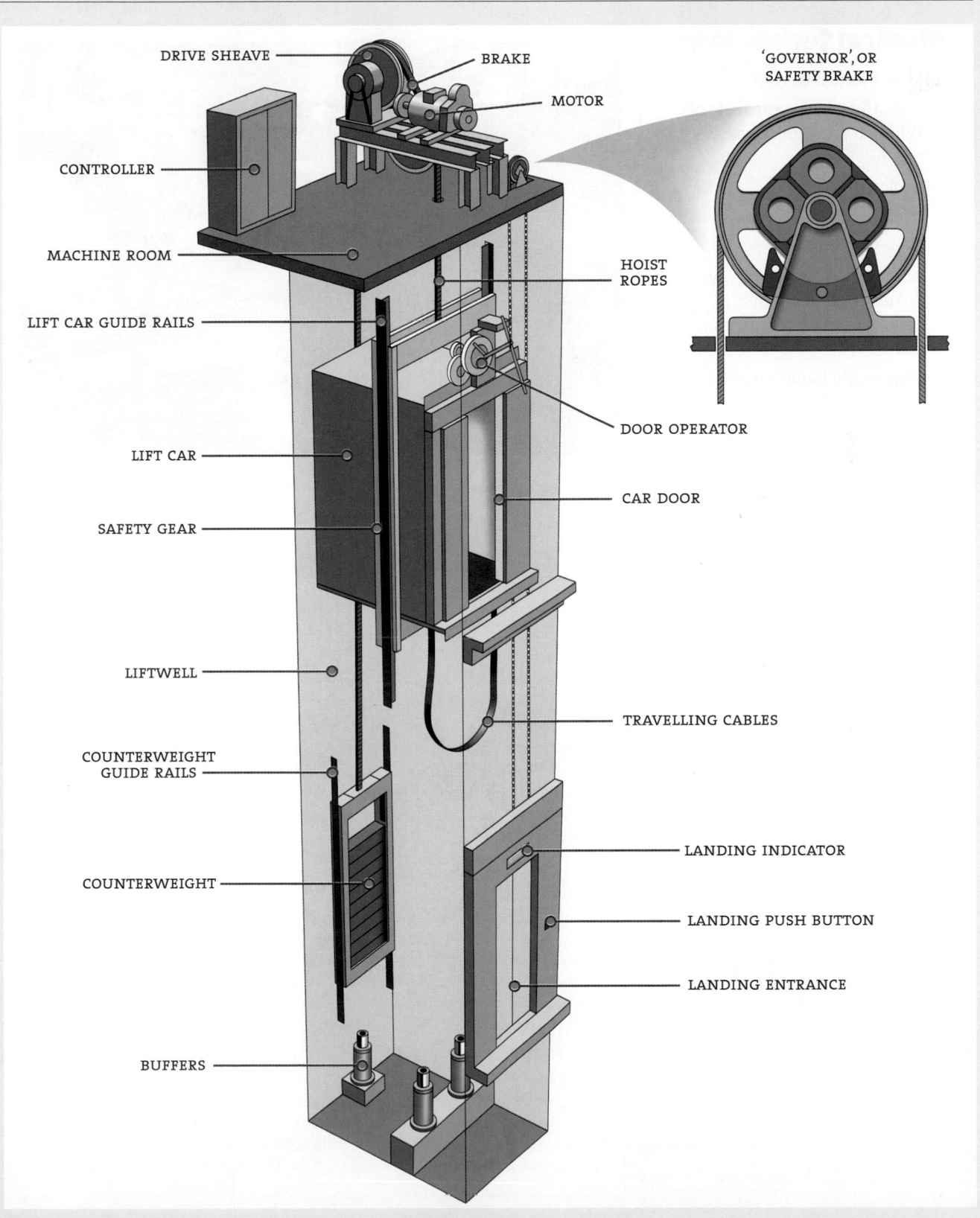

DRIVE SHEAVE

BRAKE

MOTOR

'GOVERNOR', OR SAFETY BRAKE

CONTROLLER

MACHINE ROOM

HOIST ROPES

LIFT CAR GUIDE RAILS

DOOR OPERATOR

LIFT CAR

CAR DOOR

SAFETY GEAR

LIFTWELL

TRAVELLING CABLES

COUNTERWEIGHT GUIDE RAILS

LANDING INDICATOR

COUNTERWEIGHT

LANDING PUSH BUTTON

LANDING ENTRANCE

BUFFERS

Medical technology

1 Answer the questions.

1 The affix *tele-* means 'distant'. What do you think these terms mean?

a telemedicine

b telecare

c telesurgery

2 What sort of technology would be needed for each of the services described by these terms?

3 Who might benefit from these services?

2 Read the text and check your answers.

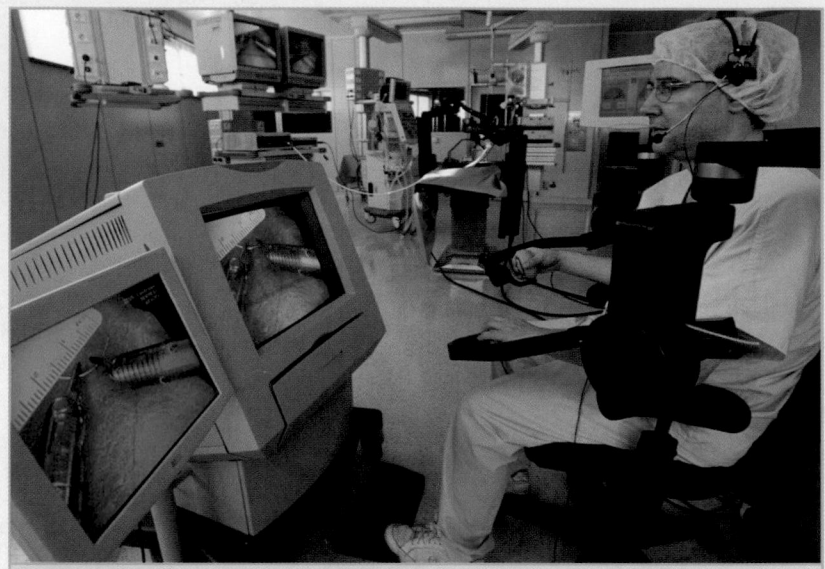

Telemedicine

Telemedicine is the application of Information Technology to medical care. It's about providing medical support at a distance to people who have no access to a doctor. Using the Internet, satellite phones, video links, and digital cameras, patients, nurses, doctors, and others can obtain specialist help quickly.

If passengers fall ill on an aircraft in flight, cabin crew can use a device called Vital signs to measure blood pressure and other important signs. The data can then be transmitted to a doctor to interpret and provide advice on treatment. Medical images, such as X-rays or ultrasound scans, can be taken in one country and sent by broadband to a specialist in another for expert advice. Using a video link, nurses in a minor injuries clinic can call a specialist to examine difficult cases remotely. This is much cheaper than having a specialist available in the clinic.

Telecare is a way of looking after vulnerable people such as old people at a distance. Sensors in their homes can detect falls, lack of activity, or even if food is removed from the refrigerator. Lack of movement triggers an alarm which alerts medical staff or relatives. Patients can wear monitors for recording the pulse and other signs. This can be sent via the telephone system to medical staff without the patient leaving home.

Telesurgery was used in 2001 to allow a surgeon in New York to operate on a patient in France. The operation was carried out using a high-speed computer link and robotic tools in the French operating theatre. At this stage, such procedures are expensive and a local surgeon has to be present in case the network link fails. In the future, however, telesurgery could be a life-saver for people living, working, or travelling remote from medical help.

Personal entertainment

1 What advice would you give to someone making a digital video movie for the first time?

2 Compare your advice with the tips given in the text.

3 Study these explanations for some of the tips given. Match each explanation to the correct tip.

a Professionals make limited use of these kinds of shots. _____

b When you start filming you won't have to worry about where to shoot next. _____

c They have to catch your attention and make their message clear in a very short time. _____

d It's quality, not quantity that counts. _____

e Unsteady or jerky shots can look amateur. _____

f If the unexpected happens on the day of filming – problems with the technology, weather, or the actors – you still have time to get it right. _____

g Wind or street noise can ruin your film. _____

h You won't lose time, or worse, make serious technical mistakes and ruin good shots. _____

i You can get all the necessary actors and locations organized in good time. _____

File Edit View Insert Format Tools Actions Help

Tips for making a digital video movie

Digital video cameras along with software such as Apple's iMovie allow anyone to make home movies. You can add video and audio effects and publish your films on websites and blogs. You can produce video podcasts for others to share. However, having the right equipment doesn't guarantee quality. These tips might help:

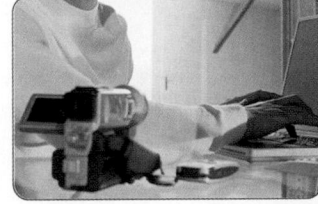

1 Prepare your storyboard well in advance.

2 Allow plenty of time for filming.

3 Make a shooting schedule listing each location and the time for filming.

4 Find quiet locations and check them before you start filming.

5 Use TV adverts for good ideas.

6 Keep your film short.

7 Make sure you are familiar with all your camera controls.

8 Use a tripod to ensure your camera is steady.

9 Don't overuse zoom shots.

Careers in technology

1 What questions would you ask someone with the job title of *Technical Installation Engineer*?

2 Read the answers to the questions the interviewer asked Ron Martinez, a Technical Installation Engineer. Correct your questions in **1** if necessary.

3 Now match these questions to the answers in the text and put them in a logical order.

  a What's the worst thing about the job? _____

  b What does your work involve? _____

  c How long have you worked there? _____

  d What advice would you give students entering your profession? _____

  e Why did you choose this job? _____

  f What's the best thing about the job? _____

  g What's the biggest challenge of your job? _____

  h What's the salary like? _____

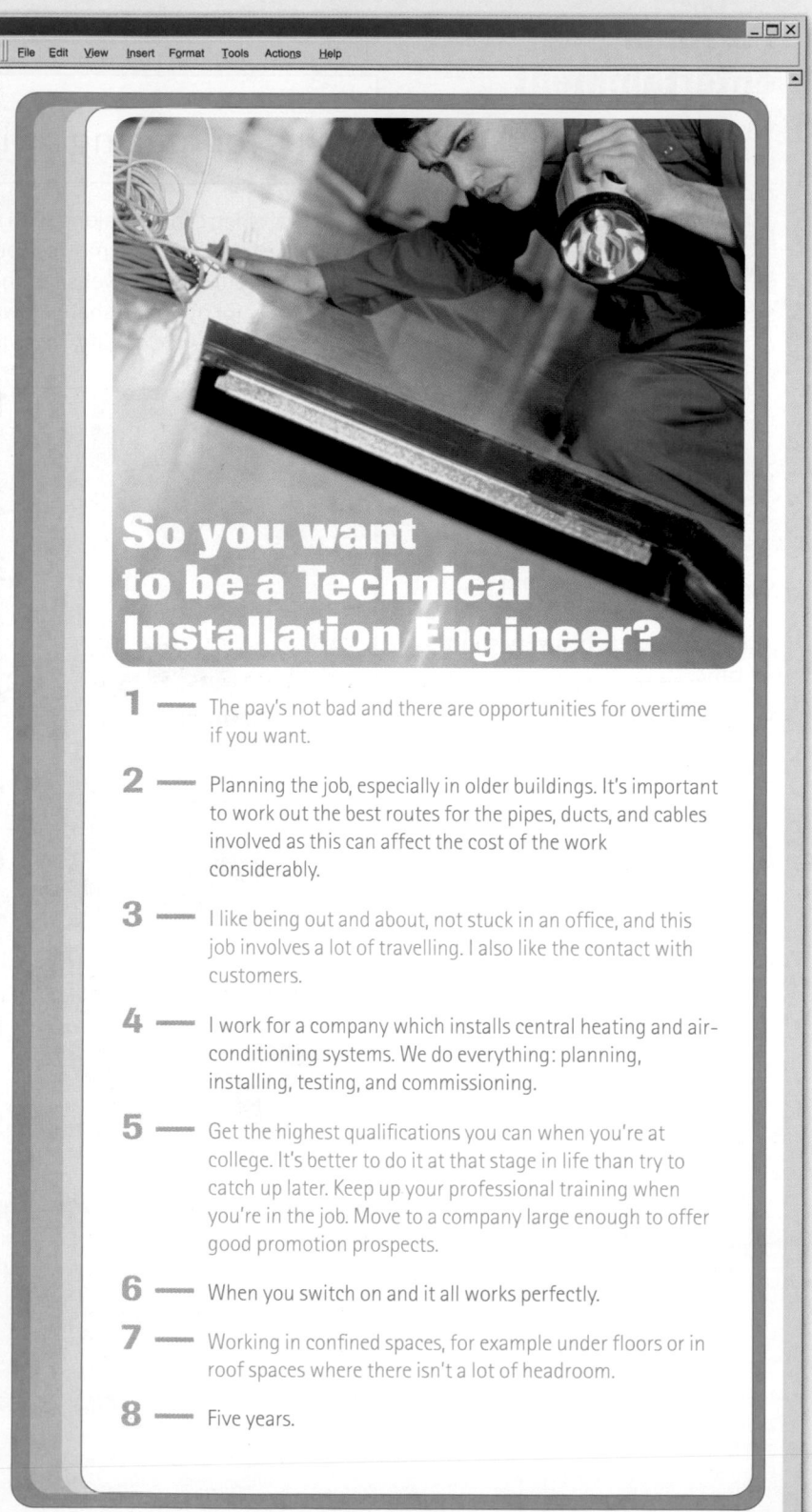

File Edit View Insert Format Tools Actions Help

So you want to be a Technical Installation Engineer?

1 — The pay's not bad and there are opportunities for overtime if you want.

2 — Planning the job, especially in older buildings. It's important to work out the best routes for the pipes, ducts, and cables involved as this can affect the cost of the work considerably.

3 — I like being out and about, not stuck in an office, and this job involves a lot of travelling. I also like the contact with customers.

4 — I work for a company which installs central heating and air-conditioning systems. We do everything: planning, installing, testing, and commissioning.

5 — Get the highest qualifications you can when you're at college. It's better to do it at that stage in life than try to catch up later. Keep up your professional training when you're in the job. Move to a company large enough to offer good promotion prospects.

6 — When you switch on and it all works perfectly.

7 — Working in confined spaces, for example under floors or in roof spaces where there isn't a lot of headroom.

8 — Five years.

The future of technology

1 For robots to function less like machines and more like humans, they need to be covered in artificial or synthetic skin. Which features of human skin does robot skin need to copy? Choose from a–d.

a sensitive to touch

b sensitive to heat

c stretchable

d all of these

2 Now read the text and check your answer.

3 Read the text again to find the answers to these questions.

1 What sorts of tasks are robots good for?

2 Typically, which industries make use of robots?

3 What do robots need in order to work with people?

4 How does E-skin stretch?

5 Why is stretchability important?

6 How could walking robots use information from E-skin in their feet?

7 How could E-skin help robots not to damage themselves?

8 What two features of E-skin would be important in bathing a baby?

Robot skin

Robots are very good at doing the same task in the same place over and over again. In factories and nuclear power stations more than a million robots behave in this way every day.

For robots to work with people, for example caring for the old, they need to be much more like humans. They need to be able to move like humans and adapt to new places. They also need to be more sensitive to touch and temperature. In humans it is skin which provides important information on pressure and heat.

Engineers at the University of Tokyo have developed an artificial skin for robots which is sensitive to pressure and temperature thanks to a large number of sensors. In addition, because it uses a mesh or net structure it can be stretched by up to 25% and still retain its sensitivity. This means it can be used to cover moving parts like joints.

This E-skin opens the way for much more sensitive robots. For example, walking robots could use feedback from their feet to adjust to different surfaces. Robots in future may be able to grasp different tools and use them as humans do. Domestic robots could pick up and bathe a baby without hurting it. They would also be less likely to damage themselves.

A lot remains to be done. E-skin will provide much more information than the robot requires at any one time. Human brains can select only the important information. Before robots can act like humans, they need to have brains like humans.

Reading bank key

Technology in sport

2

a Fastskin, Strapless goggles

b Precool vest, Power socks, Swift suit

c Power socks, Swift suit

d Fastskin, Swift suit, Strapless goggles

3

1 It reduces body temperature and therefore the risk of heat injury.

2 Because sharks are famously fast swimmers of the fish world.

3 Leg muscle vibration. The vibration is wasted energy.

4 It keeps them cool.

5 They are stuck to the eye sockets with medical glue.

Appropriate technology

1

b

2

Item	Quantity
5-metre metal or bamboo poles	3
toothed wheels	3
125 cc petrol engine	1
armour plate	2 pieces
wheel motors	3

3

1 Dervish

2 It clears anti-personnel mines.

3 It has a simple design and is cheap to make and use.

4 To create more pressure

5 After it has exploded 1,500 mines.

6 It moves in a series of tight circles so no mines are missed.

Crime-fighting and security

1

A

1 Advanced taser gun

2 Police

3 It uses compressed air to fire darts attached to electric cables. These deliver an electric shock which causes temporary paralysis.

B

1 Iris-scanning

2 Airports, banks

3 The iris is scanned digitally and the information is stored in a database. This provides a check or match when the person later requests entry to a high-security area.

C

1 Offender tracking

2 Police

3 A tracking unit records an offender's movements via GPS. A server matches these movements to places and reports automatically to the police if the offender enters forbidden areas.

Manufacturing

1 wasting: drilling

2 joining: welding

3 coating: plating

4 joining: using adhesives

5 casting: die casting

6 moulding: blow moulding

7 forming: extrusion

8 forming: forging

9 coating: powder coating

10 forming: shearing

Transport

1

Petrol engine and electric motor

2

1 Running at a constant speed, cruising

2 Low-speed cruising

3 Overtaking, hill climbing, and accelerating from stop

4 It is not necessary to plug it in to charge the batteries.

5 The electric motor serves as a generator when braking. The petrol engine also drives the generator when the batteries are low.

High living: skyscrapers

1 / 2

1 It saves energy by balancing the weight of the lift.

2 They keep the car steady and act as a safety feature.

3 Brakes on the guide rails operated by a 'governor', double-doors, multi-strand steel ropes, shock absorbers, or buffers, at the base of the lift shaft

3

1 It logs all passenger calls, monitors the number of passengers travelling from floor to floor, and the position of any car in the system and its speed. It can direct passengers to the car which will get them to their destination fastest, and will prevent any car which is overloaded from moving.

2 The large number of safety devices make it virtually impossible for an accident to happen.

Medical technology

1

1 a Administering medical help from a distance
  b Looking after people from a distance
  c Operating on people from a distance

2 the Internet, satellite phones, video links, digital cameras

3 people living, working, or travelling remote from medical help

Personal entertainment

3

a9 b3 c5 d6 e8 f2 g4 h7 i1

Careers in technology

3

a7 b4 c8 d5 e3 f6 g2 h1

Possible logical order

b4 c8 e3 g2 f6 a7 h1 d5

The future of technology

1

d

3

1 The same task in the same place over and over again

2 Factories and nuclear power stations

3 They need to be able to move like humans, adapt to new places, and be sensitive to touch and temperature.

4 It has a mesh or net structure.

5 E-skin has to cover moving parts like joints.

6 They could adjust to different surfaces.

7 The robot could detect any obstacle as soon as it touched it.

8 Sensitivity to pressure and temperature

9 High living: skyscrapers

Switch on

1 Name some famous skyscrapers. Which cities are they in?

2 Look at the diagram. It shows some of the components of a skyscraper. Match a–f below with 1–6 in the diagram.

a   concrete base

b   cladding

c   floors below ground

d   steel columns

e   horizontal I-shaped girders

f   steel piles

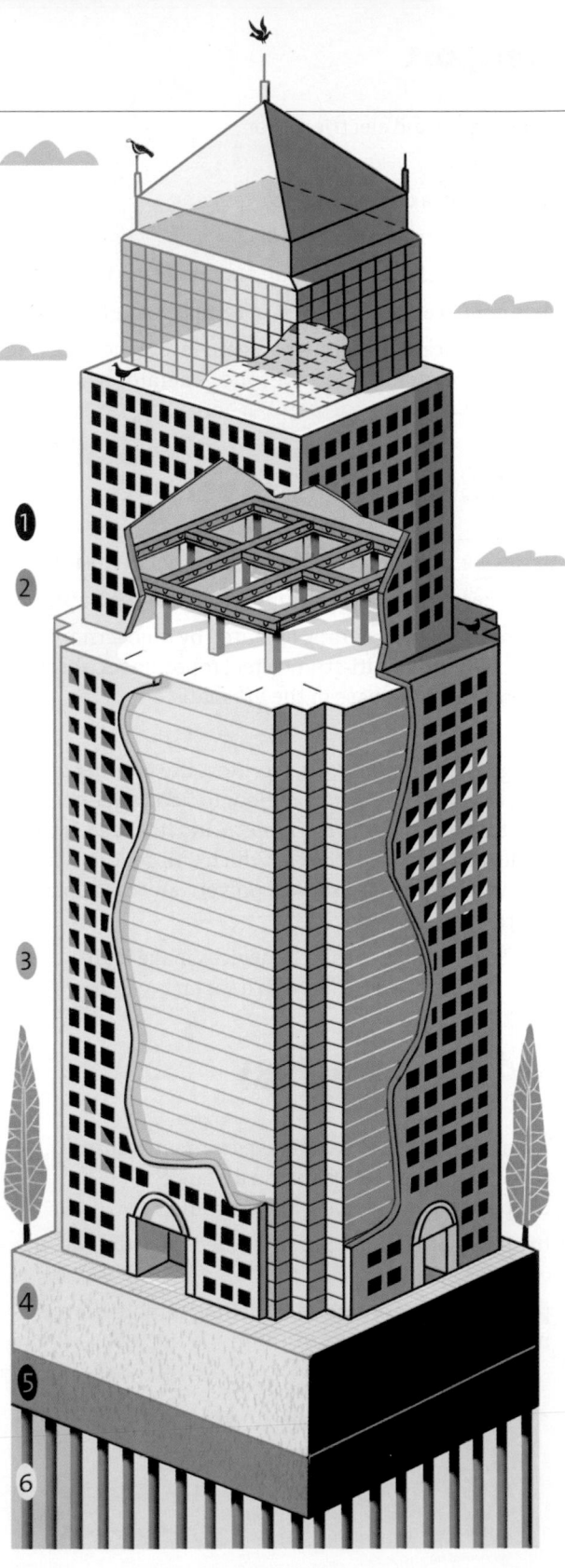

It's my job

1 🎧 Listen to Leon Peters, a Steel Erector, and answer the questions.

1 How big is Leon's gang?

2 How long is a contract?

3 What kind of buildings has he worked on?

4 What word does he use to describe components which are cut and drilled off-site?

5 How long is a typical shift?

2 🎧 Listen again and find the reasons why

1 contracts vary in length

2 bonuses are paid

3 you need good ground people

4 you don't come down for tea-breaks

5 moving girders is dangerous.

Reading

How skyscrapers are built

1 Put these stages in the construction of a skyscraper in the correct order. Then work in small groups and compare answers.

a _____ Metal decking called *floor formers* are laid across the girders to form a shallow pan.

b _____ Outer walls, called *cladding*, are lifted into position by crane.

c _____ Girders are bolted to the columns to form the floors of the building.

d _1_ The foundations are laid.

e _____ Liquid concrete is poured onto the formers.

f _____ Ducts are installed beneath each floor to carry cables and pipes.

g _____ The vertical steel columns that form the base of the building's main frame are fixed to the foundations.

h _____ The process is repeated floor by floor until the skyscraper is completed.

2 Read the text and check your answers.

Skyscraper construction

Skyscrapers start with a very large hole in the ground which will contain the foundations, several floors, and possibly even a metro or subway station. The type of foundations depend on the nature of the ground. Usually they are made by drilling narrow, deep holes and filling them with reinforced concrete to form piles. Another method is to drive steel piles, as much as twenty metres in length, into the ground. A thick raft of concrete is laid on top of the piles.

Vertical steel columns are bolted to the foundations. Each column rests on a platform of steel to spread the load. Steel girders are fixed horizontally from column to column by Steel Erectors to form a strong framework. Metal decking called floor formers are laid across the girders and filled with lightweight liquid concrete which is pumped up from the ground. When it sets, it forms the floors.

Ducts are installed below the floors to carry all services: electricity, water, drains. All exposed metalwork is fireproofed. If a fire happens, it is important that the structure can withstand high temperatures without buckling.

The same process is repeated as the building rises. In some construction methods, entire floors are built at ground level and hoisted into position by cranes.

The outside of the building is covered in cladding. This consists of prefabricated panels of materials such as stainless steel, aluminium, and glass.

The world's first skyscraper was the Home Insurance building, Chicago, built in 1885. It was only ten storeys high.

• **Language spot**
Safety signs and safety advice

• Safety signs are found on construction sites.

• Safety signs give direct commands to the reader:
No smoking.
Do not smoke here.
You must not smoke here.
Wear a safety helmet.
Safety helmets must be worn.

≫ Go to **Grammar reference** p.119

1 Match the safety signs to their meanings.

1		a	Eye protection must be worn.
2		b	In the event of fire do not use this lift.
3		c	Ear protectors must be worn in this area.
4		d	Protective footwear must be worn in this area.
5		e	High-visibility clothing must be worn in this area.
6		f	No admittance.

2 Work in pairs. Take turns to explain the signs in **1** to a trainee.

EXAMPLE
Sign 5   This means 'No admittance'. You mustn't go in there.

• More general safety advice is given in handbooks on safety and on safety training programmes:
Don't wear flammable clothing where there may be open flames.
Before operating an unfamiliar machine, check the guards.

• We use *always* and *never* to strengthen safety advice:
Check the guards before using an unfamiliar machine.
***Always** check the guards before using an unfamiliar machine.*
Don't use an unfamiliar machine without checking the guards.
***Never** use an unfamiliar machine without checking the guards.*

≫ Go to **Grammar reference** p.119

3 Rewrite the examples of safety advice using *always* or *never*.

EXAMPLE
Don't use defective tools.
***Never** use defective tools.*

1 Make sure a machine has stopped before removing the guards.
2 Do not use mobile phones in busy working areas.
3 Wear eye protection when using grinders.
4 Do not smoke near flammable substances.
5 Wear a hard hat when work is going on overhead.
6 Do not operate chain saws without ear protection.
7 Make sure the mains supply is disconnected before working on electrical equipment.
8 Store chemicals in a lockable room or container.

Customer care
Showing visitors round a construction site

1 Work in pairs. Study the picture of a group of civil engineering students who are visiting a construction site. Discuss what regulations they might be breaking and why they could be in danger.

2 The site manager is going to take the group round the construction site. Read what he says about the regulations the students must observe and note them in the table. Add reasons using the text and your own safety knowledge.

" I'm responsible for your health and safety for this visit. Have you all signed in? Construction sites are dangerous places. You must wear a hard hat and yellow vest all the time you're on site. Can you adjust the internal band of your hard hat now, please? Make sure it fits. Look up, look down. Check it doesn't fall off. "

" You've been told to wear boots. If anyone is wearing trainers or soft shoes, they can't go on the tour. There may be nails or spills anywhere. Please don't carry any loose papers with you. It's quite windy today, and I don't want papers blowing round the site. You can take pictures but no flash photography on any of the floor levels. It can distract. "

" Look out for the guys with the forklifts. Their eyes are on the load – they're not looking out for pedestrians. Don't pick anything up – it might cut or burn. Always keep with the group and make sure you sign out at the end of the tour! "

Regulation	Reason
Wear a hard hat and yellow vest.	*Construction sites are dangerous. You must protect your head and be visible at all times.*

$50m
Projected cost of the Empire state building in New York

$41m
Actual cost

Pronunciation
Stress in long words (1)

1 🎧 Listen to the words from this and earlier units. Write the number of syllables in each word.

a   aluminium   _5_
b   component   ___
c   construction   ___
d   defective   ___
e   installed   ___
f   powered   ___
g   precaution   ___
h   prefabricated   ___
i   reinforced   ___
j   skyscraper   ___
k   temperatures   ___
l   visibility   ___

2 Put the words below in columns 1–3 of the table according to their stress pattern. All the words are used in this book.

appropriate   exploration   operator
automatic   generator   polystyrene
designated   helicopter   regulation
developing   horizontal   supermarket
emergencies   kilometre   unfamiliar

1 ●●●●●	2 ●●●●●	3 ●●●●

3 🎧 Now listen and check your answers.

Pairwork

Work in pairs, A and B.

Each of you has two texts about foundation types. Match your texts to the diagrams below. Use the information to explain to your partner how these types of foundations operate.

Student A   Go to p.112.

Student B

Piles on bedrock

Reinforced concrete or steel piles which rest on bedrock. Suitable when bedrock is near the surface.

Splayed base piers

Reinforced concrete piles with expanded, or splayed, ends. These spread the weight of the building over a larger area. Used when bedrock is not near the surface but where there is a layer of firm soil near the surface.

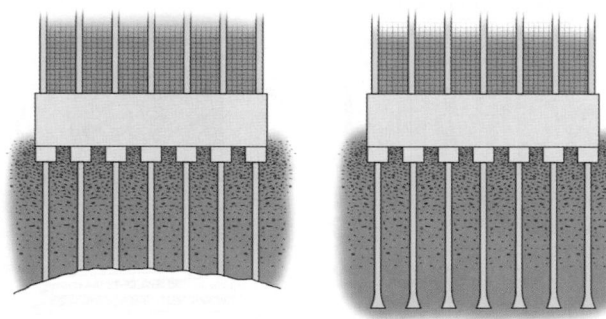

Webquest

Complete the table by finding out information about the tallest building in your country, as well as the ten tallest buildings in the world.

Country	Building name and place	Height	Floors	Year completed
Yours				
1				
2				
3				
4				
5				
6				
7				
8				
9				
10				

These sites may help:
- www.tinyurl.com/nuzdb
- www.skyscraperpage.com

Key words

Adjectives
flammable
prefabricated

Adverb
off-site

Nouns
bonus
cladding
decking
former
girder
grinder
guard
lifeline
pile
safety harness
storey

Verb
buckle

Note here anything about how English is used in technology that is **new** to you.

10 Medical technology

Switch on

1 Look at the diagram of an artificial heart system, and answer the questions.

1 What kind of patient is the artificial heart for?
2 What does the artificial heart contain?
3 Why are there *two* batteries?
4 How is the internal battery charged?
5 What is the controller for?

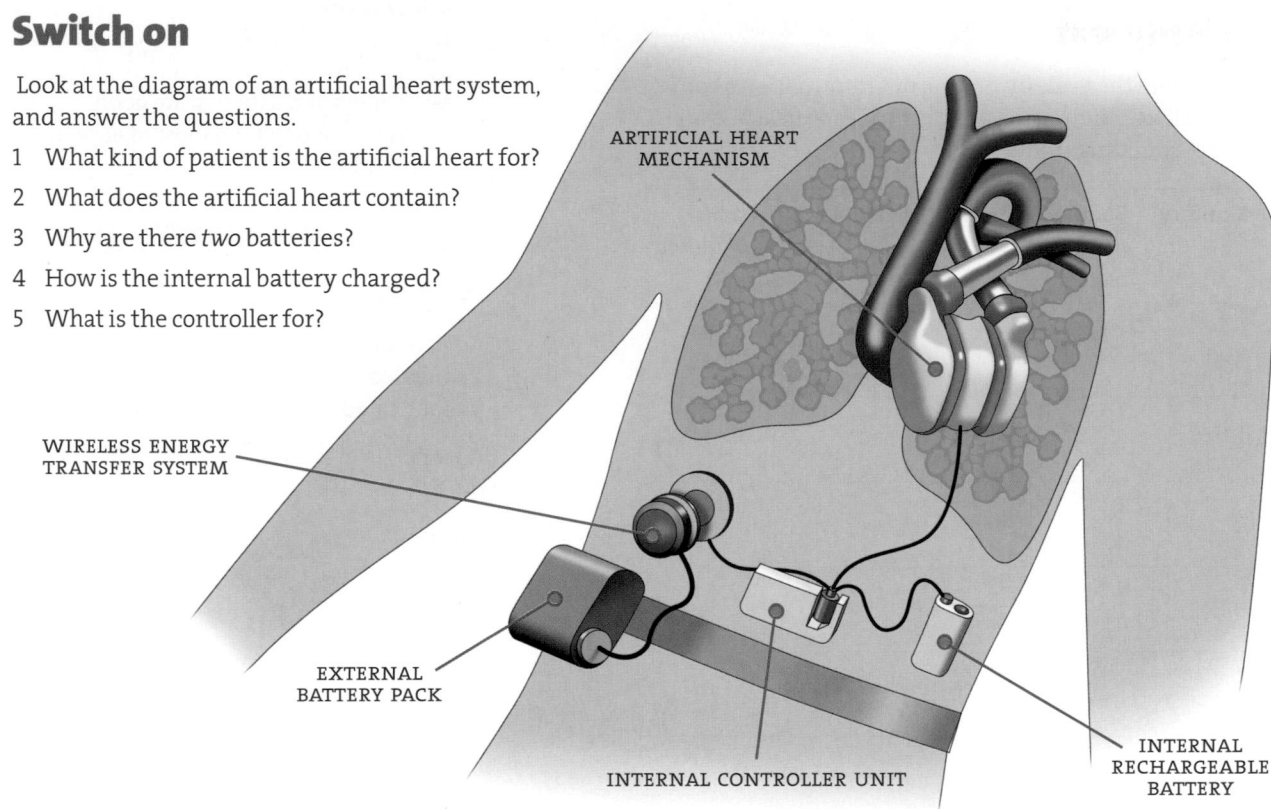

ARTIFICIAL HEART
MECHANISM

WIRELESS ENERGY
TRANSFER SYSTEM

EXTERNAL
BATTERY PACK

INTERNAL CONTROLLER UNIT

INTERNAL
RECHARGEABLE
BATTERY

2 Now read the text and check your answers.

AbioCor artificial heart

The AbioCor is an artificial heart made of titanium and plastic. It is for patients with very serious heart problems who are waiting for a heart transplant.

It contains a hydraulic pump and a valve which lets the hydraulic fluid move from one side of the heart to the other. When the fluid moves to the right, blood is pumped to the lungs. When the fluid moves to the left, blood is pumped to the rest of the body.

The system has two batteries: one internal, inside the patient's body, and one external. The internal battery lasts up to forty minutes. This is long enough for the patient to have a shower or to change the external battery. The external battery lasts four to five hours.

The external battery provides power using a wireless energy transfer system. A coil on the patient's skin induces power in a coil inside the body. This operates the controller and charges the internal battery.

The controller contains a microprocessor which decides the best heart rate for the patient at any time.

It's my job

1 Before you listen, discuss with your partner possible answers to the questions.

1 What is E A T ? (A = Assistive)

2 Name three ways in which severely disabled people can operate equipment.

3 What are the three branches of engineering which make up *mechatronics*?

4 What does a *page-turner* do?

5 How does a *pneumatic switch* work?

2 🎧 Now listen to Phillipe Rugeri, a Mechatronics Engineer, and check your answers.

● Language spot

Relative clauses

● Study these examples:
A pacemaker is a device for people.
The people have heart problems.

● We can join these sentences like this:
*A pacemaker is a device for people **who have heart problem**s.*

● The part in **bold** is a relative clause. It adds important information – defining or telling us exactly who the people are. In the relative clause you replace *The people* with *who*. *Who* is used for a person or people.

● Now study these examples:
A page turner is a device.
The device turns the pages of books or magazines.

● We can join these sentences like this:
*A page-turner is a device **which turns the pages of books or magazines**.*

Which is used for things.

» Go to Grammar reference p.120

1 Make definitions of each person or device in column A of the table by matching them with the information in column B.

EXAMPLE
1 *A hearing aid is a device which helps deaf people.*

A		B
1 hearing aid		applies engineering principles to medical problems
2 X-ray technician		helps people with damaged kidneys
3 X-ray camera		people can use to call for help in an emergency
4 lab technician		takes 3-D images of the brain and other organs
5 kidney machine	person who	helps people who cannot walk
6 personal alarm	device which	helps people with heart problems
7 bioengineer		works in a scientific laboratory
8 CAT scanner		helps deaf people
9 pacemaker		specializes in taking and processing X-rays
10 wheelchair		takes pictures of bones and organs in the body

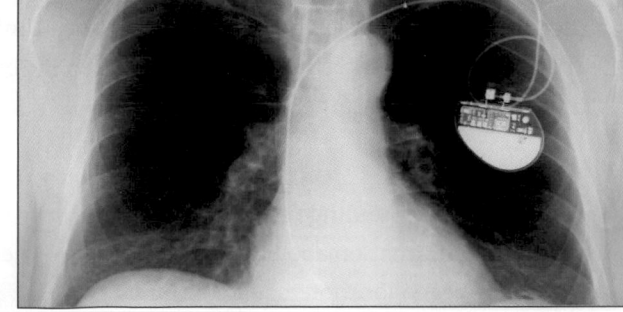

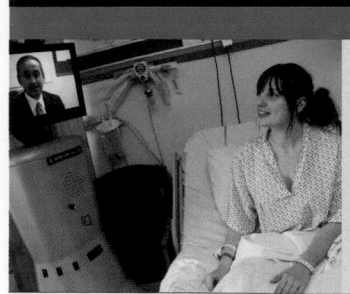

Gadget box

RP6 (Remote Presence) is the UK's first robot doctor. It allows doctors anywhere in the world to communicate directly with patients in their hospital beds. The robot is controlled by the doctor using a joystick. It is fitted with a camera so that the doctor can examine the patient.

What are the advantages and disadvantages of the robot doctor?

2 Look at the pictures of the Ultracane. Who do you think will use it? How do you think it works?

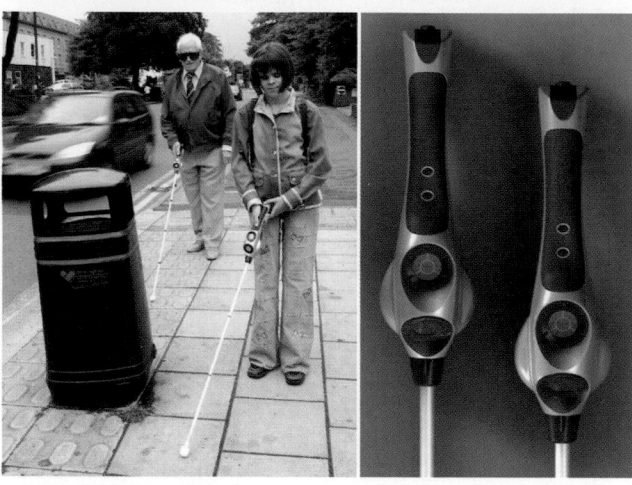

3 Fill the gaps in the description of the Ultracane with information a–g. Add *who* when the information describes people. Add *which* for things.

a invented the cane

b calculates the position and size of the object

c are near the blind person

d have tried the cane

e helps blind people to avoid obstacles in their path

f cannot see well

g are for objects in front and overhead

Problem-solving

Put devices a–e in order of how useful they are to a blind person (1 = most useful, 5 = least useful). Then work in small groups and compare your answers. Try to agree on the best order.

a a scanner which reads books and documents out loud _____

b a voice-operated computer _____

c a global positioning device which tells you where you are with an accuracy of ± 3 metres _____

d a fridge which reports when food is past its sell-by date _____

e software which allows your computer to read onscreen information out loud _____

Useful language

Disagreement
I don't really agree with you.
I don't think you're quite right.

Agreement
That sounds like a good idea.
I think so too.

Persuasion
Isn't X more useful than Y?

Blind people or people _____[1] often use a cane to feel their way when walking. The Ultracane is a new type of cane _____[2]. It uses echo-location, like a bat, to detect objects around the blind person. Some people call it the *Batcane*. The cane transmits ultrasound signals. These are reflected by objects _____[3]. Sensors on the cane receive the reflected signals which are passed to a microprocessor _____[4].

There are four buttons on the handle of the cane – the two _____[5] are on the top, and the two which are for objects on the left and right are on the back. These buttons vibrate when an object is detected. The larger the object, the larger the vibration.

People _____[6] say that with a little practice they can use these vibrations to make a mental map of their surroundings as they walk. Because the cane uses vibrations, not noise, they can also use their ears for additional information about their surroundings. The engineers _____[7] are now planning new uses of echo-location to help the blind.

Vocabulary

Opposites

When a word and its opposite are often used together, try to remember them as a pair. Complete the missing words (they are all used in this book).

1	backwards	a	_____
2	_____	b	anticlockwise
3	_____	c	external
4	input	d	_____
5	open	e	_____
6	_____	f	step-down gear
7	wind /aɪ/	g	_____

Customer care

Giving clear instructions

One way of communicating with customers is by instruction manuals or leaflets for your company's products. These need to be written in clear, simple language which cannot be misunderstood. This is particularly important in medical technology, where there is a high degree of risk to the user or damage to the product if it is used wrongly.

1 Study the extract from instructions for using a medical inhaler. Discuss with your partner if these instructions are easy to understand and follow.

> ## How to use your inhaler the right way
>
> *Using an inhaler may seem simple, but many patients do not use their inhaler in the right way. If you use your inhaler the wrong way, less medicine goes to your lungs. For the first two weeks, read these instructions out loud as you follow them.*
>
> ### Getting ready
> 1 Take off the cap and shake the inhaler.
> 2 Breathe out all the way.
> 3 Hold your inhaler in the correct way (see picture).
>
> ### Breathe in slowly
> 4 As you start breathing in slowly through your mouth, press the inhaler down once. (If you use a spacer, press down on the inhaler first. Then within five seconds start to breathe in slowly.)
> 5 Take as long a breath as you can, slowly.
>
> ### Hold your breath
> 6 Hold your breath and count slowly to ten.

2 Study the description of how to charge the batteries for an electric wheelchair. Use it to make a set of clear instructions for a wheelchair user. Give titles to the steps of your instructions.

> The batteries must be charged when the capacity has fallen to 10%. This is indicated by two **red** lights flashing at the top of the joystick. When the charger is connected, a **yellow** charging indicator will show on the control panel. When the **green** indicator lights, this shows that the batteries are fully charged. Batteries should be charged in a well-ventilated area using only the charger supplied.

3 Exchange your set of instructions from **2** with another student and decide if it can be followed easily. Mark any places where the instructions are not clear enough.

If somebody a few years ago saw the medical technology
we make now, they'd call us miracle workers.
Dr J W Steadman
Institute of Electrical and Electronics Engineers

Pronunciation

Linking words

When a word begins with a vowel sound, the final
consonant sound of the word before links to it.

1 🎧 Listen to this example.
a door opener

2 Mark where the words link in compound nouns 1–10.
Then read them out loud.

1	a curtain opener	6	a domestic appliance
2	a window opener	7	a gear box
3	a personal alarm	8	a diesel engine
4	a remote control	9	a digital radio
5	a light switch	10	an MP3 player

3 🎧 Listen and check your pronunciation.

Writing

Short description

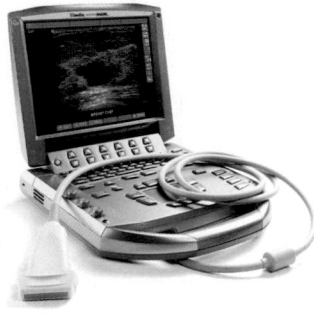

1 Study the information
about an ultrasound
machine, which makes
images of internal parts of
the body. Use it to complete
the short description
on the right.

Main components	Function
transducer probe	generates, transmits, and receives high-frequency sound waves
piezoelectric crystals	produce sound waves when current is applied across them
Computer	
CPU (central processing unit)	processes the data from the transducer to produce an image
hard disk storage device	stores the image along with patient details and other information
LCD monitor	displays the image

keyboard	allows the operator to key in patient details and other information
printer	prints the image

An ultrasound machine is used to _____
_____[1]. It consists of a transducer
probe, computer, LCD monitor, keyboard, and
_____[2]. The probe
contains _____[3]
which _____[4].
The computer includes a CPU which _____
_____[5]. This is displayed on _____
_____[6]. It also contains a hard disk
which _____[7]. This information
is keyed in on the _____[8].
Images can be printed or copied to DVDs.

2 Find out about CAT scanners (CT scanners), and write
your own description in the same way.

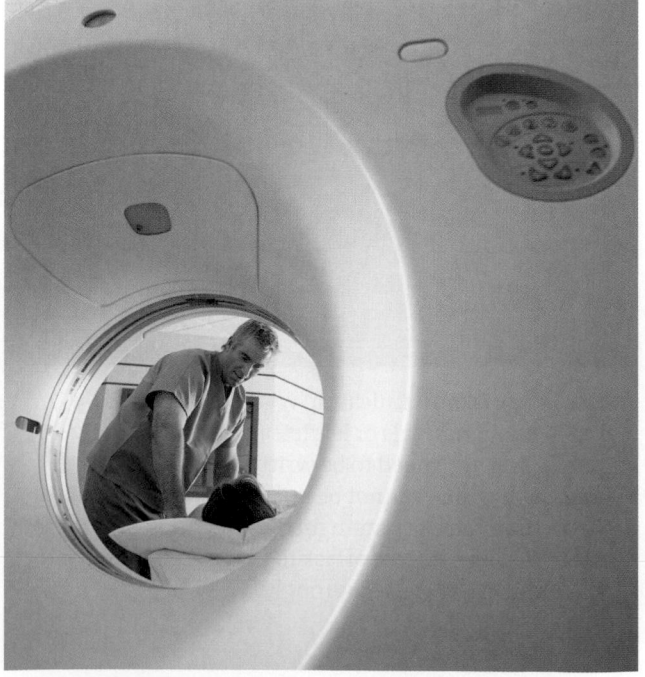

Pairwork

1 Work in pairs, A and B. Discuss ways in which technology could provide a safe environment for an elderly person living alone and make a list.

2 Each of you has a list of devices produced by a company specializing in telecare for the elderly. Make notes in the table and then describe to your partner what you think these devices are for, and how they work.

Student A   Go to p.112.

Student B

Device	a) What it's for	b) How it works
Pressure-sensitive floor tiles		
Movement detector		
Pillow alert smoke alarm		
Temperature extremes sensor		
Personal radio alarm trigger		
Bogus caller button		

3 Choose from your combined lists the six most important devices to ensure a safe environment for an elderly person living alone.

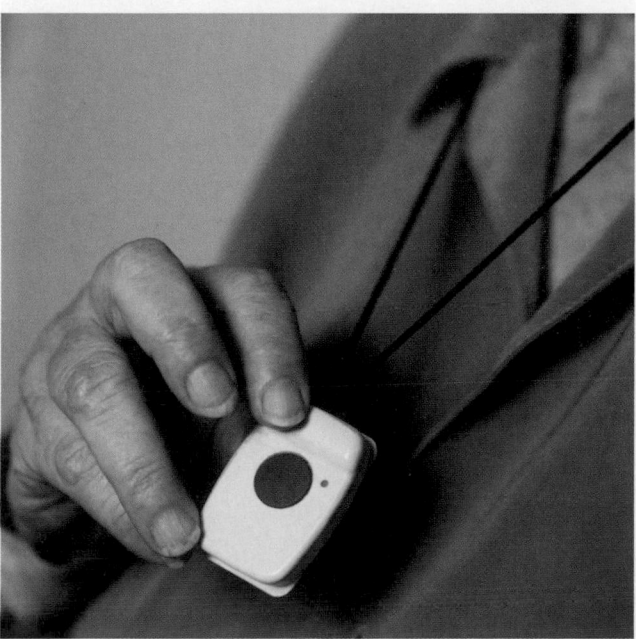

Checklist

Assess your progress in this unit.
Tick (✓) the statements which are true.

☐ I know key terms in medical technology

☐ I can make definitions with relative clauses

☐ I can locate information in a diagram and text

☐ I know how to link words when speaking

☐ I can write a short description

☐ My reading and listening are good enough to understand most of each text in this unit

Key words

Adjectives
artificial
hydraulic
rechargeable

Nouns
accuracy
coil
image
joystick
scanner
sell-by date
ultrasound
valve
web page

Verbs
calculate
reflect
vibrate

Note here anything about how English is used in technology that is **new** to you.

11 Personal entertainment

Switch on

Do a class survey. Find out how students in your class listen to music, apart from live performances. Then complete the table with the percentage.

Device	Percentage of students
Radio	
TV	
CDs	
Online	
Portable hard disk devices	
Other portable devices	

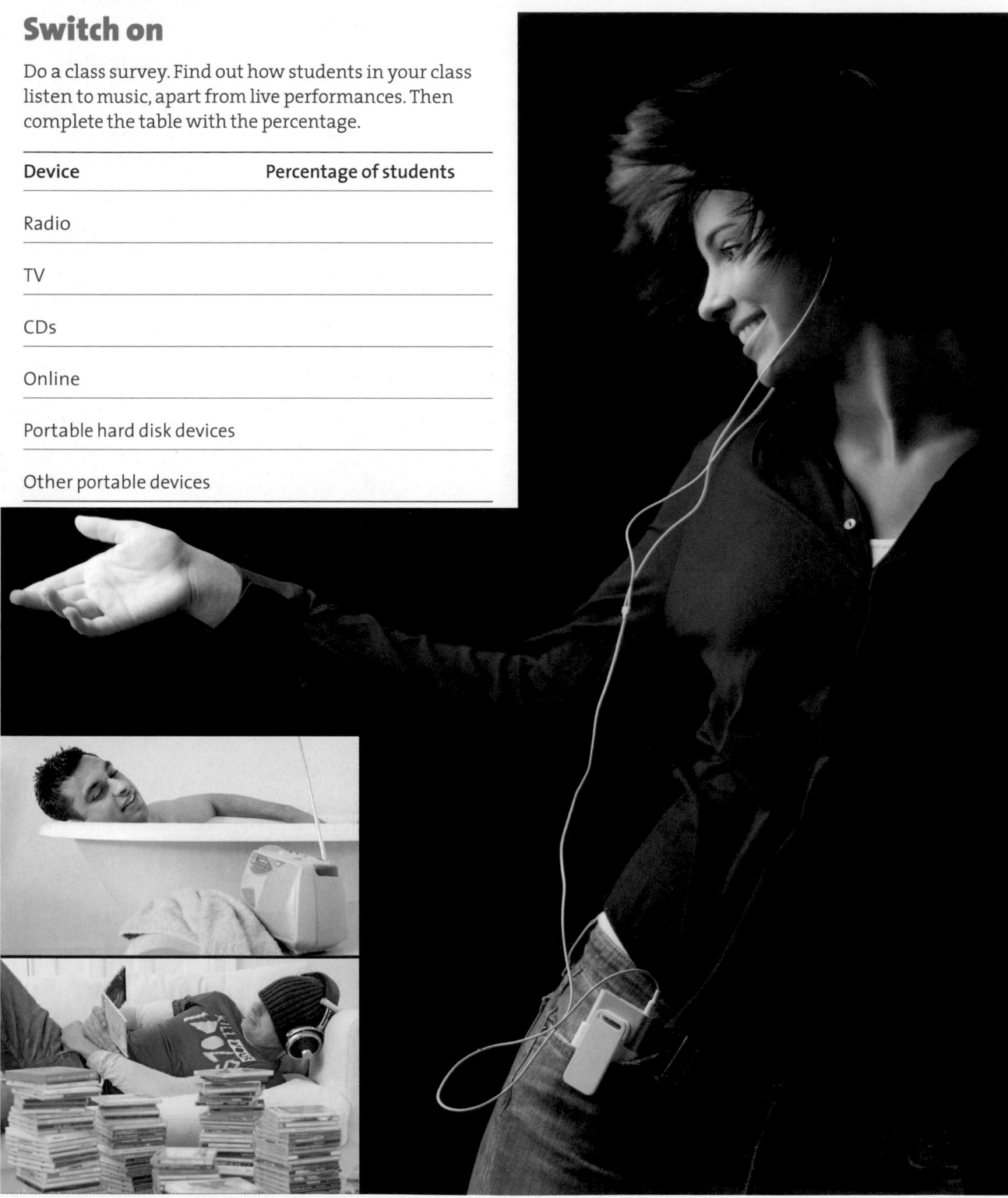

In this unit
- key terms for personal entertainment devices and video games
- listening for opinions
- how to give advice using *should / shouldn't*
- using your reading skills to find information about video games

Listening

Opinions

1 🎧 A radio interviewer is discussing developments in online music with Max Eggers, who works in the music industry, and Sam Fassbinder, a student. Listen and note how Max and Sam listen to music.

Max

_____

_____

_____

_____

Sam

_____

_____

_____

_____

2 🎧 Listen again and answer the questions.

1 Which music services does Max use?
2 According to Sam, what's special about this way of listening?
3 How many people regularly download music from illegal sites in Britain?
4 What does Max think of this?
5 How is it damaging the music industry?
6 What does Max think the music industry should do?
7 What does Sam think of this?

● Language spot

should / shouldn't

● Study these examples:
*What **should** the music industry do?*
*They **should** go after anyone who downloads illegally.*
*I don't see why we **shouldn't** share tracks with our friends.*

● We use *should* and *shouldn't* to give advice and to express opinions. Often we use *I think* before advice to show it's our personal opinion:
*I **think** you shouldn't play violent video games.*

>> Go to **Grammar reference** p.120

1 Complete the sentences with *should* or *shouldn't* and the words in brackets.

1 (You / download) _____ tracks from illegal sites. It damages the music industry.
2 (You / use) _____ Napster or iTunes. They're legal and they offer a wide range of music.
3 If you want quality pictures, (you / buy) _____ a digital camera with fewer than 3.3 megapixels.
4 I think (you / share) _____ tracks with friends. It's illegal.
5 I don't think (you / buy) _____ a VCR. They're out-of-date. Buy a DVD player.
6 (You / give) _____ your password to anyone.
7 (You / update) _____ your virus protection software.
8 It's easy to damage a flat screen. (You / touch) _____ it.

2 Sam has a job interview tomorrow with a large engineering company. Give her advice using *should* or *shouldn't* and notes 1–10.

1 Be late.
2 Dress smartly.
3 Practise answering questions with a friend.
4 Be honest. Exaggerate your skills.
5 Prepare some questions of your own.
6 Read up as much as you can about the company.
7 Look at the floor when you speak.
8 Look at all the interviewers.
9 Lean back and look bored.
10 Sit straight and look confident.

CGI (n) Computer-generated imaging
demo (n) a demonstration game

It's my job

1 Read about Bruno Schleef, a Video Games Designer. Make a list of the jobs he mentions, and note the kind of work they do.

EXAMPLE	JOB	WORK
	Level Designer	*scripts events*

2 Read about Bruno again and answer the questions.

1 Why is it difficult to get a job in the video games industry?
2 What qualifications does Bruno have?
3 How did he get a demo?
4 Name two predictions he makes about video games.
5 What other applications does video games technology have?

Webquest

Find out more about working in the video games industry. Make notes about the following information.

- education / qualifications
- experience
- salary

Compare answers with other students in your class. These sites may help:

- www.gamesindustry.biz/jobs.php
- www.gamejobs.com

Bruno Schleef: Video Games Designer

It's difficult to get into this industry because you have to show success, and you can't do that without having experience.

I took a degree in Computer science, worked for a while, and then did a Master's in Computer games technology. We got into a competition called 'Dare to be digital' as a team of five students. Our team won the prize for 'Greatest marketing potential'. That got us noticed and gave us a **demo**. So that's how I got started.

Another way in is to be a Games Tester. It's the hard way. You play games for eight hours a day, trying to make them fail. But quite a lot of people have become Level Designer from that position. You can script events in the game.

I work as part of a development team. A few years ago you only needed a couple of Programmers and an Artist. Now we've got teams of sixty or more. In addition to Games Designers like me who are responsible for creating ideas for games, there are Concept Artists. They're normally trained Illustrators who draw 2-D characters. There are 3-D Artists who do all the 3-D modelling. There are also 3-D Animators who make the characters move. Of course, you have your Producer – to oversee, make sure deadlines are kept, and the work goes to budget, that kind of thing. You've got your Programmers to write the code. If you want realistic slow-motion action, you need **CGI** experts.

The way it's going is more film techniques are coming into games. More people are getting broadband so online playability is important. Massively multiplayer online gaming, MMOG. That's also proving really popular and is sure to grow. They're role-playing games you play online with other people. As other hardware, mobile phones, all that stuff, becomes more advanced, what you play your games on will become less specific, not just consoles. You can play online at home, then plan your next moves on your mobile phone on your way to work.

It all sounds good fun, but there's a serious side to games, too. Companies make military simulations and medical simulations, for example, dealing with a neck injury, responding to a disaster.

Vocabulary

New vocabulary

1 Entertainment technology is creating a new use for old words. Match the words with their definitions.

1	burn	a	copying tracks to CDs from online music sites
2	rip	b	recording your CDs and encoding them into MP3 or other digital files
3	tag	c	broadcasting files, mainly audio, on the Internet for others to download
4	podcast	d	adding extra information about artists, albums, and songs to tracks on your MP3 collection

2 Do you know any other new vocabulary connected with entertainment technology? If so, work in pairs and explain the words to your partner.

Problem-solving

1 Study the pie chart showing the best-selling computer game genres in the USA, and answer the questions.

  1 What genre of computer games sells most?

  2 What genre sells least?

  3 What do you think a *strategy* game is?

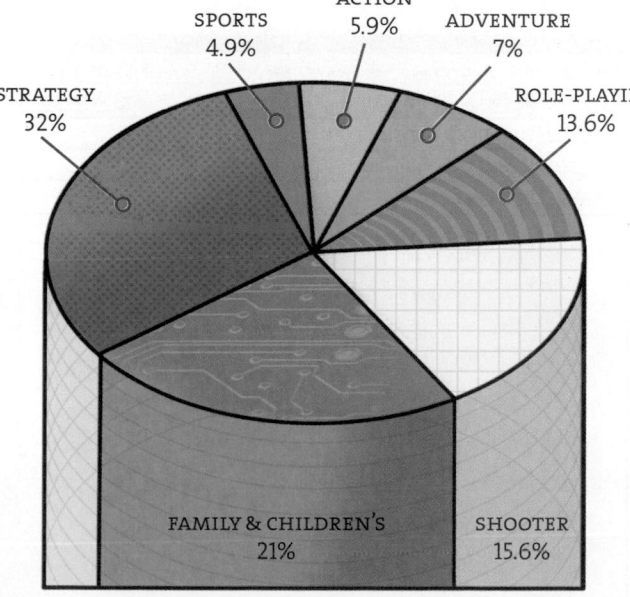

2 Work in pairs. Using the title, decide which genre each of the games belongs to. Explain the reason for your answers.

1	Jade Empire	*role-play*
2	Charlie and the Chocolate Factory	_____
3	Grand Theft Auto: San Andreas	_____
4	The Sims	_____
5	Stronghold	_____
6	Doom 3	_____
7	Pro Evolution Soccer	_____
8	Legend of Zelda	_____

The US Society of Hand Therapists warns that excessive use of handheld electronic devices can lead to hand and wrist problems. Some of these have been called *Texter's thumb*, *Blackberry cramp*, and *iPod finger*.

Customer care
Making suggestions

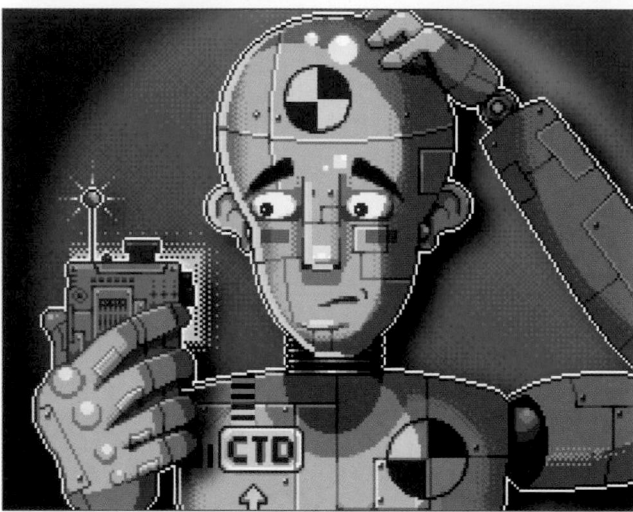

1 Sam has a problem downloading a music file, so she contacts Customer support. Read her email.

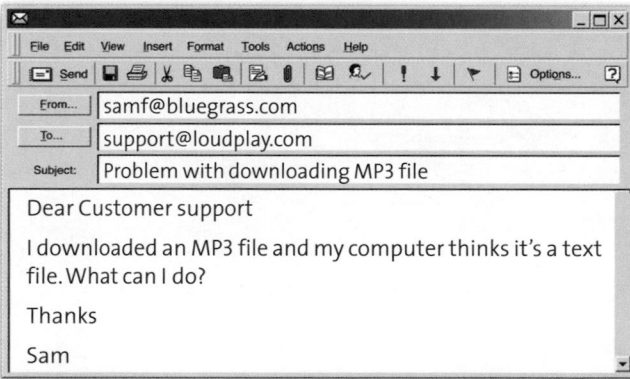

File Edit View Insert Format Tools Actions Help
Send   Options...

From... samf@bluegrass.com
To...   support@loudplay.com
Subject: Problem with downloading MP3 file

Dear Customer support

I downloaded an MP3 file and my computer thinks it's a text file. What can I do?

Thanks

Sam

2 Read how Customer support replies to Sam.

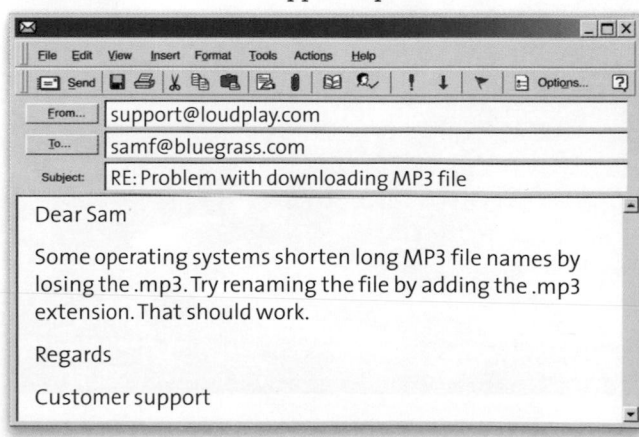

File Edit View Insert Format Tools Actions Help
Send   Options...

From... support@loudplay.com
To...   samf@bluegrass.com
Subject: RE: Problem with downloading MP3 file

Dear Sam

Some operating systems shorten long MP3 file names by losing the .mp3. Try renaming the file by adding the .mp3 extension. That should work.

Regards

Customer support

3 Reply to the customer enquiry and make suggestions using the notes below.

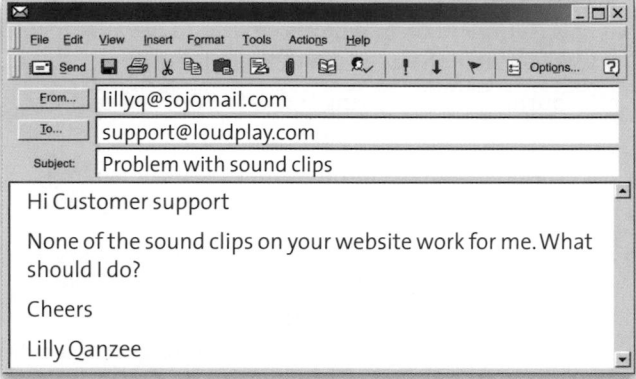

File Edit View Insert Format Tools Actions Help
Send   Options...

From... lillyq@sojomail.com
To...   support@loudplay.com
Subject: Problem with sound clips

Hi Customer support

None of the sound clips on your website work for me. What should I do?

Cheers

Lilly Qanzee

All clips are in Windows Media format – customers must have Windows Media Player installed.
If they have Windows Media Player installed, they should:
check their system sound settings
check the sound settings on their media player
(The sound settings might need to be turned up.)

Useful language

Do…
You can do…
Try doing…
I suggest you do…

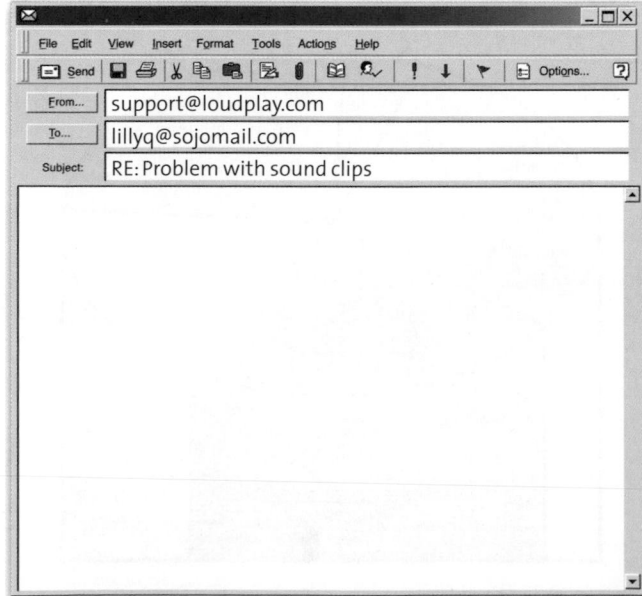

File Edit View Insert Format Tools Actions Help
Send   Options...

From... support@loudplay.com
To...   lillyq@sojomail.com
Subject: RE: Problem with sound clips

Pairwork

Work in pairs, A and B. Each of you has details of a video game. Exchange information with your partner by asking and answering questions and complete the table.

Name of the game	
Company / Development team	
Type of game	
Console	
Good features	

Student A Go to p.112.

Student B

Gran Turismo 4
This is a driving simulator game. You can buy, modify, and race cars. It was developed by Polyphony Digital for Sony. This version is for the PlayStation 2 console. The best features are the graphics, which are very realistic, and the driving, which is very accurate.

Checklist

Assess your progress in this unit.
Tick (✓) the statements which are true.

☐ I know key terms in personal entertainment technology

☐ I can give advice in a number of ways

☐ I can listen for opinions

☐ My reading and listening are good enough to understand most of each text in this unit

Key words

Adjectives
online
portable

Nouns
animator
broadband
clip
code
games console
hard disk
hardware
program
setting
simulation
track
trend

Verb
update

Note here anything about how English is used in technology that is **new** to you.

12 Information technology

Switch on

1 Look at the pictures. What uses for information technology can you think of in these places or situations?

2 Match the examples of computer use in column A with the areas of application in column B. More than one answer is sometimes possible.

A
1 using barcodes to identify items and prices
2 calculating the exact distance to a target
3 producing scale models of new designs
4 identifying an employee by his or her voice
5 checking credit cards used for payments
6 issuing seat numbers
7 analysing blood tests
8 storing employee records
9 keeping a record of all borrowings
10 calculating the stress on a component
11 controlling the temperature of a washing machine
12 monitoring the safety of each stage in the process
13 warning when aircraft are too close
14 monitoring the life signs of a patient
15 comparing fingerprints
16 co-ordinating information from all parts of a war-zone

B
a hospital
b airport
c supermarket
d design
e security
f library
g military
h oil refinery
i the home

3 Now list the uses for computers in an area of technology you are familiar with.

Reading

CADCAM

1 Look at the pictures below. What uses for computers in car production can you see?

2 What do you think terms 1–4 mean? Read the text and check your answers.

1 CAD   2 CAM   3 CNC   4 CIM

3 List the things computers can do in the design and production of a car.

EXAMPLES
allow 2-D and 3-D designs to be made
calculate dimensions from a design

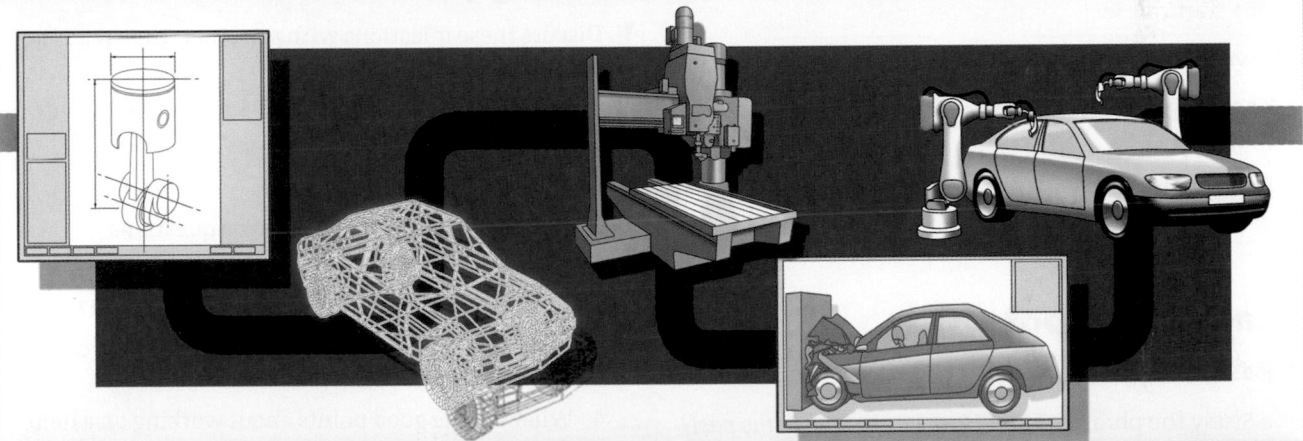

COMPUTER USE IN THE CAR INDUSTRY

All products begin with an idea. In the past, car designers worked first on paper. At a later stage models were made in wood or fibreglass. Now everything is done using CAD (Computer-aided design) programs. These programs allow designers to work in two or three dimensions (2-D or 3-D) but most new designs are created using a solid modelling program which allows the model to be viewed from any angle. It can also be viewed by engineers and executives anywhere in the world.

The models have accurate dimensions and the design files can be sent to rapid modelling devices to produce a prototype. Before a single component is produced, programs will have worked out the forces acting on it. Crash conditions can be simulated to test the safety features of the car. Assembly can be simulated to work out the best way of building the car. This saves time and money.

For components such as engine parts, when the design is complete, the file is imported into a CAM (Computer-aided manufacturing) program. Here, all machining operations are planned. The file is then sent to a post-processor which converts the data into a set of instructions in a form which can be read by Computer numerical controlled (CNC) machine tools. These instructions are fed to a CNC controller which controls the machine tools which shape the finished product.

In complete Computer-integrated manufacturing (CIM), computers control the assembly line and monitor the supply of materials, ordering new supplies when needed. They can calculate when tools need to be replaced. Computers also permit changes in a product to be made easily. Orders can be customized to meet the needs of a particular client. 'Special editions' of cars can be produced to attract new customers to a model, for example the BMW Mini.

On the assembly line, computer-controlled robots are used for tasks such as welding and painting. Robots with sensors check the finished vehicle for defects. For example, they can check the paint thickness and how well the doors fit.

The name was first suggested by a colleague. We'd been in the meeting for hours and, while he was drinking a cup of Peet's Java coffee, he picked 'Java' as an example of yet another name that would never work. The initial reaction was mixed.

Arthur van Hoff
former Senior Engineer, Sun Microsystems

4 Complete column B of the table.

A How was it done in the past?	B How is it in the present?
1 designs produced on paper	
2 dimensions calculated by measuring	
3 models made by hand	
4 real cars crash-tested	
5 supplies ordered by staff	
6 welding done by hand	
7 painting done by workers	
8 cars inspected by people	

● Language spot

Past Passive

● Study the phrases under *How was it done in the past?* in the table in *Reading* **4**. We can make each phrase into a sentence like this:

Designs *were produced* on paper.

● We use the Past Passive to describe actions in the past where the action is more important than the agent performing the action, or where the agent is not known.

>> Go to **Grammar reference** p.121

1 Make each phrase from column A of the table in *Reading* **4** into a sentence using the Past Passive.

2 Link each pair of phrases, past and present, into one sentence.

EXAMPLE

1 *Designs were produced on paper but now they are produced by CAD programs.*

Listening
Describing changes

1 🎧 Laura Santini works for a company which makes cans and containers for the food and drink industry. She explains to a journalist some of the changes which have taken place in this industry. Listen and note the six changes she describes.

2 🎧 Work in pairs and compare your answers. Then listen to the recording again.

It's my job

1 Discuss these questions with a partner. Then read the text to check your answers.

1 What kind of work does an IT Support Technician do?

2 What is a *help desk*?

2 Read the text again and answer the questions.

1 How did Diana find her first job?

2 What makes working on a help desk difficult?

3 What words does Diana use to describe how callers to the help desk feel?

4 What are the good points about working on a help desk?

5 Why is it not a good idea to work on a help desk for long?

6 What are the attractions of Diana's new job?

7 What information sources does Diana use in her work?

8 How will Microsoft certification help Diana?

3 Find an expression in the text which means:

a people-handling skills

c working directly with people

b problem-solving

d dealing with telephone calls.

Diana Mayo:
IT Support Technician

I'm an IT Support Technician. I work for a large chain which sells building materials to the public and to tradespeople. Almost every business these days, large or small, needs support technicians.

When I left college, I got a job through an agency working for a company which provided online support to local businesses and individuals. I was on their help desk. That meant taking calls and providing advice on all sorts of problems. It's a job where you need not just technical skills but also good 'soft skills'. That means people-handling skills. You need to be able to understand how the caller feels as well as trying to solve their IT problems. You have to keep calm when you're under pressure. People may be pretty frustrated by the time they phone you, and they expect you to fix their problem right away. It's a demanding job because you have to cope sometimes with angry people, get all the information you need to help them with their problem, work out how to solve it technically, and then explain in a clear, simple way what they can do to put things right.

A help desk is a good place to start. You learn to think quickly and how to handle people but I wouldn't advise doing it for long. It's not the best paid job. In my present job I get to work with people face-to-face. The work is more interesting. It's not all trouble-shooting. I also get to install software, maintain servers, and advise on the best choice of new hardware. The money is better too. I find the best way to find information on problems is to use the Internet. Most of the manufacturers have sites which provide information. There are also newsgroups for sharing information.

I'm planning to get Microsoft certification. My company is prepared to pay for the courses and the exams. It's good for them as it means I can do more and it's good for my future.

Customer care
Working on a help desk

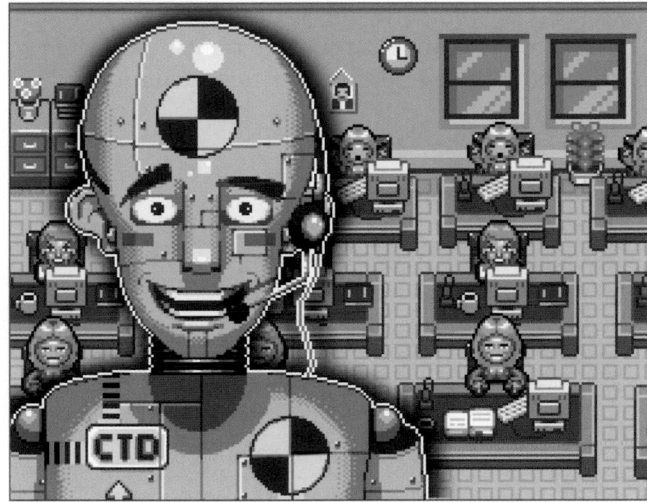

Some computing support technicians work on help desks like Diana. They take telephone calls from people with IT problems. They have to:

- record the facts about the problem accurately
- diagnose the problem
- provide the right advice.

1 Study this extract from a problem report form. Find out the meaning of any unfamiliar terms.

Item	
Location	
Make	
Model	
Problem	
Advice given	
Cleared by phone	Yes / No
Requires visit	Yes / No

2 🎧 Now listen to the recording and complete as much of the form as you can.

3 Work with a partner. With the help of the completed form take turns at playing the role of the help desk technician and the person needing help.

4 Compare your performance with the Listening script on p.128. What differences do you notice between your version and the Listening script?

Computers in the future may have only 1,000 vacuum tubes and weigh no more than 1.5 tons.
Popular Mechanics, March 1949

peripherals (n) secondary equipment connected to a computer

Vocabulary
Collocations

1 Collocations are words which are often used together. The verbs in column A are used in computing. Match them with an appropriate noun from column B.

EXAMPLE
download + pictures

A	B
click on	a menu
calculate	an icon
download	a page
display	pictures
create	the Web
scroll up / down	costs
surf	a new document
select from	information

2 Now cover **1** and fill the gaps in the sentences.

1 Flat screens around the airport display _____ on all arrivals and departures.

2 Click on the _____ for PowerPoint to prepare a presentation.

3 You can download _____ from your camera.

4 Spreadsheets are used to calculate _____ .

5 Scroll down the _____ until you find the information you need.

6 I normally spending at least one hour a day surfing _____ .

7 She created _____ to keep track of software updates.

8 You can select from the _____ to choose which application you need.

Pronunciation
-ed form of verbs and words with silent letters

The *-ed* form of verbs is pronounced in three ways:
/t/   /d/   /ɪd/

1 🎧 Listen to words 1–15. All the words are used in this book. Put them in the correct columns of the table.

1 constructed	6 finished	11 planned
2 controlled	7 integrated	12 produced
3 customized	8 invented	13 reflected
4 damaged	9 mixed	14 searched
5 disabled	10 operated	15 worked

/t/	/d/	/ɪd/

2 🎧 Now listen and check your answers.

3 Can you work out a rule to help you decide how to pronounce other *-ed* forms?

4 Words 1–7 contain silent letters. Cross out the silent letters.

EXAMPLES   cou~~l~~d   desi~~g~~n

1 listening	4 pneumatic	7 would
2 might	5 should	
3 modelling	6 vehicle	

5 🎧 Now listen and check your answers.

Speaking
Computer peripherals

1 Work in pairs, A and B. Each of you has pictures of four computer **peripherals**. Find out which peripherals your partner has by asking questions. Don't ask directly for the names of the peripherals.

EXAMPLE

A *What shape is it?*
B *It's square.*
A *Does it have a back and front?*
B *Yes, it does.*
A *Is it used for ... ?*

Student A   Go to p.111.

Student B   Go to p.112.

2 When you have identified the peripherals, together decide whether they are input or output devices.

Webquest

Find out about the five fastest supercomputers in the world and complete the table. Compare your answers with others in your class.

Order	Type or name	Speed	Maker	Location
1st				
2nd				
3rd				
4th				
5th				

This site may help:
- www.top500.org

Checklist

Assess your progress in this unit.
Tick (✓) the statements which are true.

- [ ] I know key terms for computer use in the car industry

- [ ] I can use the Past Passive

- [ ] I know how to pronounce the *-ed* form of verbs and words with silent letters

- [ ] My reading and listening are good enough to understand most of each text in this unit

Key words

Adjectives
customized
simulated
three-dimensional (3-D)
two-dimensional (2-D)

Nouns
assembly line
CADCAM
CIM
CNC
defect
machine tool
machining
peripheral
software
supplies

Verb
inspect

Note here anything about how English is used in technology that is **new** to you.

13 Telecommunications

Switch on

1 Work in small groups. List as many ways as you can to send and receive messages.

EXAMPLE

1 *by phone*   2 *writing*

2 Identify the devices used in telecommunications in pictures A–F.

3 Work in pairs. Choose one device each and explain to your partner what it does.

EXAMPLE

A *I'll choose the space satellite.*

B *OK. What does it do?*

A *It follows an orbit in space. Some satellites help communication and others provide information …*

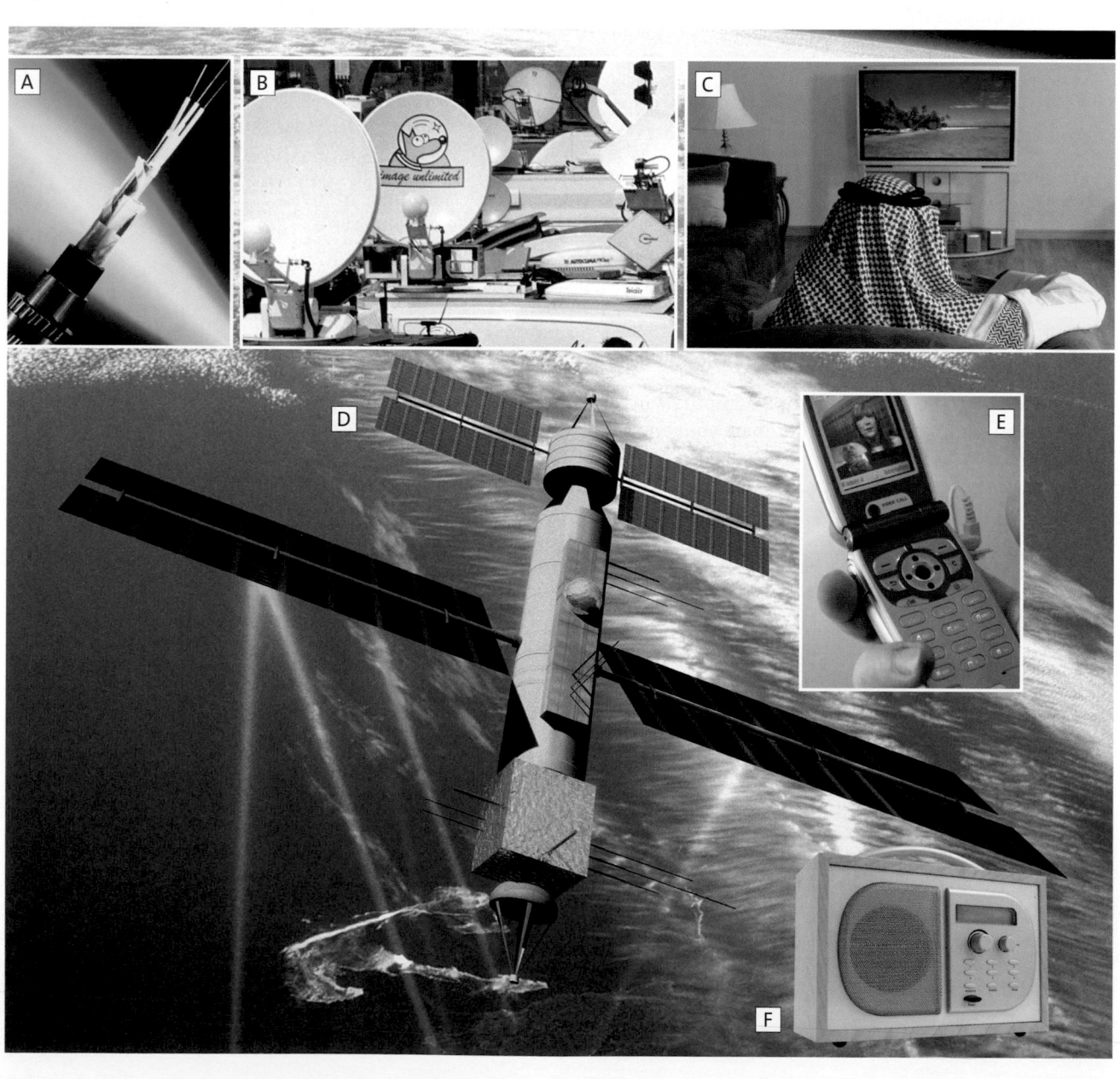

In this unit
- Past Simple v Present Perfect
- hearing the difference: Past Simple v Present Perfect
- key terms in telecommunications
- listening and reading for detail
- making simple explanations

It's my job

1 🎧 Listen to Todd McArthur, a Telecommunications Technician. Note the following things.

1 the number of years he has worked for his company

2 as many items of telecommunications equipment as you can

3 as many country names as you can

4 the meaning of VoIP

2 🎧 Listen again and answer the questions.

1 Where did he first learn about telecommunications?

2 Name a change he has experienced in telecommunications.

3 Why is his job now much more about brain than muscle?

4 What does he like most about his job?

5 What does he not like?

● Language spot

Past Simple v Present Perfect

● Study these examples from *It's my job*. Why is the Past Simple used for sentences 1–3 and the Present Perfect for sentences 4–6?

1 *I was in the army for four years.*
2 *I joined when I left school.*
3 *I travelled quite a lot.*
4 *I've been with the company for eight years.*
5 *I've been to Norway, Kenya, and Belize.*
6 *I've seen quite a few changes in phone systems.*

● We use the Past Simple for things that happened at a particular time in the past or during a period that ended in the past:
*I **travelled** a lot when I was in the army.*

● We use the Present Perfect to talk about past experiences but not when they happened:
*I've **been** to the USA.*

● We use the Present Perfect for actions which happened during a period from the past to the present:
*He's **worked** as a technician for eight years. (He's still a technician.)*

● We often start a topic using the Present Perfect and then switch to the Past Simple:
A *Have you ever **been** to Norway?*
B *Yes, I **went** there in 2001.*

≫ Go to **Grammar reference** p.121

1 Complete the text about developments in radio and television. Put the verbs in brackets in the correct form, Past Simple or Present Perfect.

In just over a hundred years, radio _____[1] (develop) into a major form of entertainment and communication. Marconi _____[2] (invent) a wireless telegraph system in 1896. This _____[3] (be) the birth of radio. Voice transmission _____[4] (start) in 1909 following the invention of the valve. Semiconductors _____[5] (make) it possible to develop much smaller, portable radios. The introduction in recent years of digital radios _____[6] (allow) us to enjoy much better sound quality.

There _____[7] (be) many changes in television too. In the UK, the BBC _____[8] (start) daily TV broadcasts in 1936. Colour broadcasts _____[9] (begin) in the late 1960s. Since the 1970s satellite broadcasting _____[10] (allow) viewers a wider choice of programmes. The recent introduction of digital TV _____[11] (mean) better picture and sound quality. Manufacturers _____ now _____[12] (develop) entertainment systems which include television, radio, DVD recorder / player, and computer. The Internet _____[13] (make) it possible to enjoy radio and television from around the world on our PCs.

Gadget box

Japan's DoCoMo network allows users of 3G mobiles to use their phones as electronic wallets. The phone acts as a credit card. When the phone is passed over a special reader, it can pay for things and allow money to be withdrawn from a cash machine. As well as password protection, some phones using the system have a fingerprint scanner.

Why do you think a fingerprint scanner is useful with this system?

2 Choose the correct alternative.

Interviewer	How long *have you been / were you*[1] a Telecommunications Technician?
Todd	About ten years. I *have trained / trained*[2] in Signals when I was in the army.
Interviewer	How long *have you been / were you*[3] in the army?
Todd	I *have served / served*[4] for four years. Then I *have joined / joined*[5] this company about eight years ago.
Interviewer	*Have you seen / Did you see*[6] many changes during this time?
Todd	Yes, *we've replaced / we replaced*[7] copper lines with fibre-optic cables and *we've introduced / we introduced*[8] VoIP phone systems.

Pronunciation

Past Simple v Present Perfect

🎧 Study these pairs of sentences. You are going to hear one of each pair. Tick (✓) the one you hear.

1 a They've spent time in the army.

 b They spent time in the army.

2 a I've texted him an invitation.

 b I texted him an invitation.

3 a He faxed me a reply.

 b He's faxed me a reply.

4 a Todd's phoned the office.

 b Todd phoned the office.

5 a She emailed me twice.

 b She's emailed me twice.

Speaking

Mobile phones

Work in pairs, A and B. Each of you has information about a mobile phone. Exchange information with your partner by asking and answering questions and complete the table.

Student A   Go to p.113.

Student B

	A	B
Make		HP
Model		iPaq hw6510 Mobile Messenger
Keyboard type		full Qwerty
Screen		3 inch, 64K
Software		Windows Mobile 2003
Other features		GPS satellite navigation
		Bluetooth
		voice control, SMS (text) and MMS (picture) messaging
Email		instant messaging

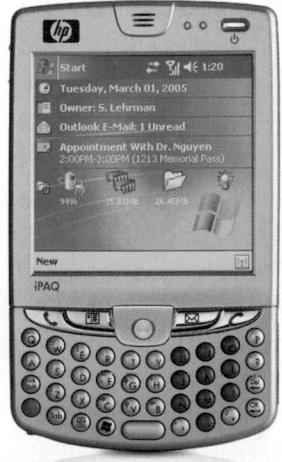

First telegraph message, 1844: *What hath God wrought?*
('What has God done?') Samuel Morse
First telephone message, 1876: *Mr Watson, come here, I want you.* Alexander Graham Bell
First email message, 1971: test signal, not preserved.

Reading

VoIP phone systems

1 Work in pairs and answer the questions. Then read the text and check your answers.

1 What does VoIP stand for?

2 What is a *packet*?

3 What is a *wireless hotspot*?

How VoIP phone systems work

VoIP (Voice over Internet Protocol) phone systems work by sending data via the Internet in tiny packets. This is called packet switching. It works like this:

1 Your voice signal, which is analogue, is converted into digital data. If you have a standard phone, you need an extra piece of hardware to do this called an ATA (Analogue telephone adaptor). If you have an IP phone, it produces a digital signal so you don't need an adaptor. You can also use your PC and a microphone as a telephone.

2 The sending computer uses software to compress the digital data, much like MP3 files.

3 The data is divided into packets, each one 30 milliseconds long.

4 The packets are sent to a router which decides the best path through the Internet for each packet. They will travel by many different paths. They will arrive at different times and some may even be lost.

5 The receiving computer uses special software to store the packets and put them in the right order. Because the packets are so small, you won't hear the difference if some are lost.

6 The data is converted back to voice and played through your standard phone, IP phone, or PC headphones.

If you have a wireless VoIP handset, you can make and receive calls anywhere near a wireless hotspot. Some mobile phones are dual-mode. You can use a mobile phone network or wireless VoIP, depending where you are.

2 Put the steps in the correct order to make a flowchart showing how this type of VoIP phone system works.

a The packets are sent to a router.

b The digital data is compressed by the sending computer.

c The data is converted back to voice.

d The receiving computer puts the packets back together again.

e The voice signal is converted to digital.

f The digital data is divided into very small packets.

g The router sends each packet through the Internet by the best available path.

1   _e_   3 _____   5 _____   7 _____

2 _____   4 _____   6 _____

geosynchronous (adj) describing satellites which orbit at the same speed as the earth but may not be above the equator. Some have figure-of-eight orbits.

Customer care
Explaining in simple terms

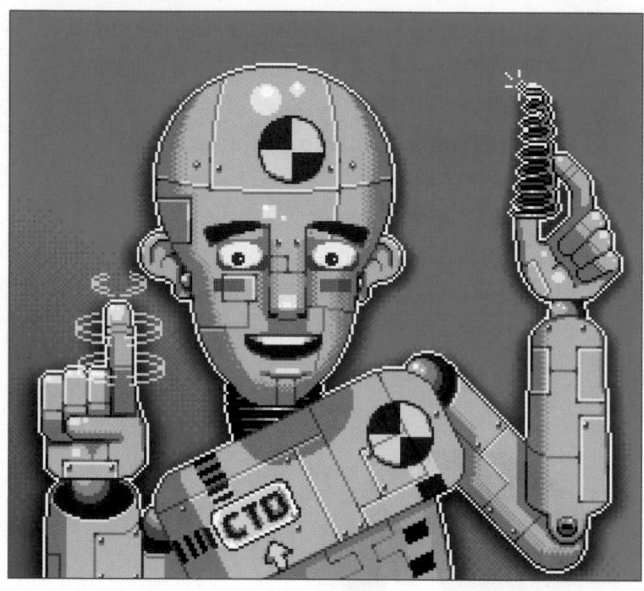

1 Like Todd McArthur, you may have to explain to clients in simple terms a process, or what a device is for and how it works. Work in pairs, A and B. Find out more about your device or process, then explain it in simple terms to your partner.

Student A   the difference between analog and digital signals

Student B   the difference between DVDs and CDs

Useful language
Basically …
In general …
To put it simply …
In very simple terms …
The main thing is …

These sites may help:
- www.howstuffworks.com
- www.wikipedia.org

2 🎧 Now listen to a native speaker explaining the differences. Compare your explanation with his. What differences can you find in the language used and the points made?

Webquest
Satellite communciation systems

1 Study the diagrams, which explain geostationary orbit. Then answer questions 1–4.

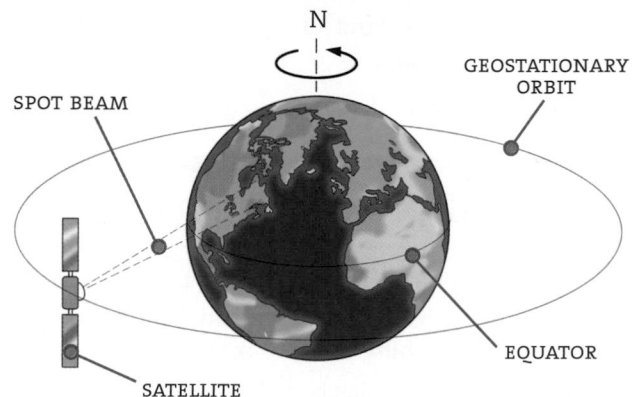

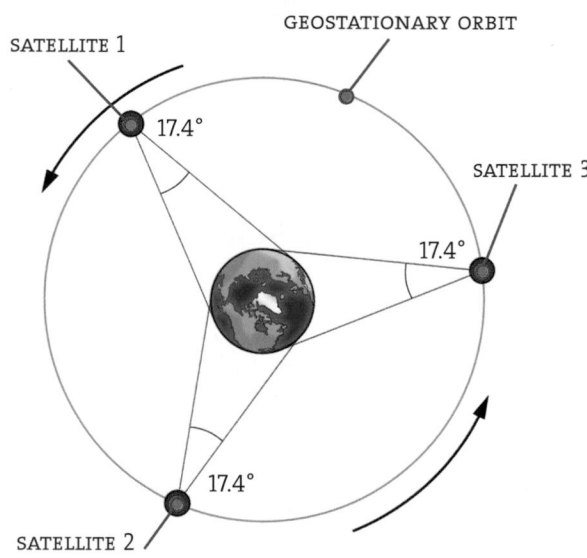

1 How long does a satellite in geostationary orbit take to rotate round the earth?

2 How many satellites in geostationary orbit are required to provide global coverage?

3 Why is it an advantage to launch geostationary satellites from countries near the Equator?

4 What are communications satellites used for?

2 Study the information about Milstar.

System	Milstar
Used for	US military communications
Number of satellites	5
Altitude	41,200 km
Orbit	**geosynchronous**
Coverage	global

3 Find out similar information about one of these satellite communication systems and complete the form below.

SES Astra

Eutelsat

Worldspace

System	
Used for	
Number of satellites	
Altitude	
Orbit	
Coverage	

These sites may help:

- www.wikipedia.org
- www.eutelsat.com
- www.ses-astra.com
- www.worldspace.com

Key words

Adjectives
compatible
complex

Adverb
in orbit

Nouns
adaptor
antenna
computer file
dish
network
router
satellite
screen
semiconductor
wireless hotspot

Verbs
compress (data)
replace

Note here anything about how English is used in technology that is **new** to you.

14 Careers in technology

Switch on

1 Choose two jobs from the list of jobs in technology that you would like to do. Then choose two which you would not like to do.

Aerospace Engineer
Agricultural Engineer
Biomedical Engineer
Chemical Engineer
Civil Engineer
Electrical Engineer
Electronic Engineer
Environmental Engineer
IT Engineer
Marine Engineer
Materials Engineer
Mechanical Engineer
Nuclear Engineer
Petroleum Engineer
Public Health Engineer
Sound Technician
Special Effects Technician
Telecommunications Technician
Transport Engineer

2 Work in small groups, and explain your choices.

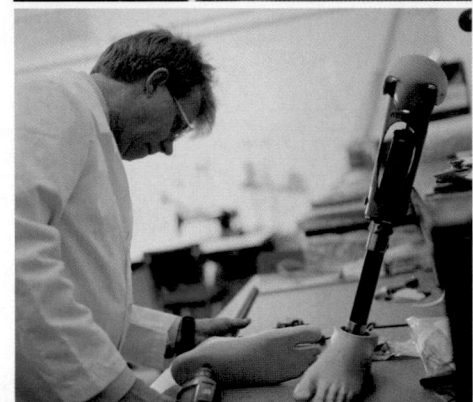
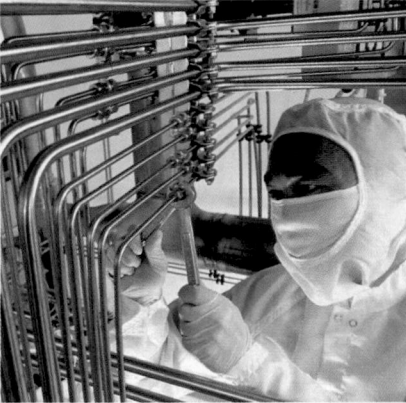

In this unit
- discussing and reading about jobs in technology
- how to describe job requirements
- writing a CV
- interview skills

Reading
Job descriptions

Work in groups of three. Choose one job description (A–C) each. Make notes about the job. Then describe the job to others in your group using only your notes.

Your notes should cover:

1 the job title and some of the areas covered
2 what you think are the most important requirements
3 the location of the work
4 good and bad points about the job.

B

Telecommunications Technician

Your work could involve:
- Making, testing, and checking components
- Assembling equipment
- Installing, setting up, testing, and repairing equipment
- Laying and connecting cables
- Installing radio equipment and mounting antennas on buildings or on masts

You could work inside in a factory or outside working in all weather conditions. Your work could involve lifting and working at heights.

Requirements

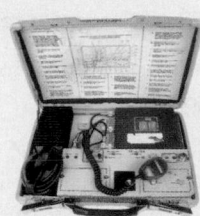

Essential:
- degree or diploma in IT
- physical fitness

Desirable:
- good communication skills
- good teamworker

A

CIVIL ENGINEER

You could work in any of these fields at any point from the design to the completion of the structure:

Construction	buildings, sports stadiums, shopping centres
Transport	railways, roads, bridges
Power	hydro-electric schemes, dams, pipelines
Hydraulics	the movement of water from one area to another
Maritime	the construction and development of docks and harbours
Public health	waste disposal and sewage treatment plants

You might work both in offices and on site. Site work can be in difficult areas far from any town or city.

REQUIREMENTS

Essential:	– degree or diploma in civil engineering
	– ability to think creatively
Desirable:	– look at things in a practical way
	– enjoy problem-solving
	– good teamworker

Sound Engineer

You could work in recording studios making high quality sound recordings, mainly for the entertainment industry. Sound engineers operate complex electronic equipment to reproduce music, dialogue, sound effects, and other audio content.

Your work could cover all types of sound for:

COMMERCIAL MUSIC RECORDINGS
THEATRE, RADIO, FILM, AND TV
WEBSITES
VIDEO AND COMPUTER GAMES
MULTIMEDIA

Requirements

Essential:	degree or diploma in an appropriate discipline
	excellent hearing
	a real interest in music and technology
Desirable:	ability to work long hours
	a co-operative and friendly attitude
	good organizational skills

Competition for sound engineering jobs is fierce. You have to be willing to work long hours for little pay at first.

C

£50,000–£70,000
€74,000–€104,000
$93,000–$131,000

Typical annual salary range in 2005 for Offshore Petroleum Engineers (with experience) in the UK

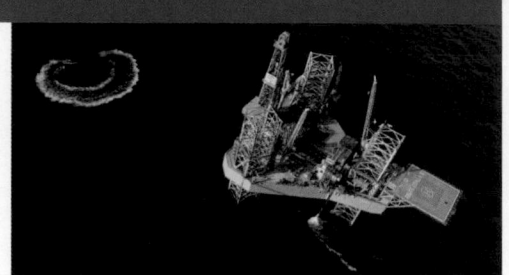

● Language spot

Job requirements

● We can describe **essential** requirements like this:
You **must** *have a degree or diploma in IT.*
You **must** *be physically fit.*

● Note the meaning of the negative form:
You **mustn't** *be colour-blind. (It's a requirement* **not to be** *colour-blind.)*

● We can describe **desirable** requirements like this:
You **should** *have good organizational skills.*
You **should** *be able to cope with long hours.*

>> Go to **Grammar reference** p.122

1 Write sentences to describe the requirements for jobs 1–3.

(✓✓ = essential, ✓ = desirable, ✗ = requirement not to be)

1	**Satellite Technician**
✓✓	diploma in engineering
✓✓	good team player
✓	good communication skills
✓	physically fit
✗	afraid of heights
✗	colour-blind

2	**Engineering Construction Technician**
✓✓	certificate or diploma in engineering
✓✓	good mathematical and computing skills
✓	willing to travel
✓	able to explain complex requirements in clear terms

3	**Offshore Petroleum Engineer**
✓✓	diploma or degree in petroleum engineering
✓✓	willing to travel
✓✓	willing to spend long periods in difficult environments
✓	good communicator
✓	able to supervise others

2 List the essential and desirable requirements for this job.

WESTGATE THEATRE

STAGE TECHNICIAN

Westgate theatre is seeking to appoint a Trainee Stage Technician to join a backstage team based in London.

Candidates should preferably have a certificate or diploma in an area such as:
– *Electrical engineering*
– *Electronics*
– *Audio-visual communication*

Other technical areas will be considered.

Practical skills in carpentry and construction would be an advantage. Candidates must be prepared to work irregular hours and to travel. Theatre experience an advantage but not essential.

 Information and application packs can be downloaded from **www.westgate-theatre.co.uk** or send a CV and covering letter to:

Kasia Johns
Westgate theatre
1 Maxwell Court
London WC2A 5DD

CLOSING DATE FOR APPLICATIONS IS FRIDAY 13TH OCTOBER 20–

3 Find out what the job requirements are for a career you are interested in.

This site may help:

● www.connexions.gov.uk/jobs4u

Writing

CV

1 Study the CV. It is based on the European Curriculum Vitae format.

PERSONAL INFORMATION

Name	Aisha Q. Chetty
Address	7 Linden Crescent, Edinburgh, EH3 7DP, United Kingdom
Phone	(+44) 131 123 4567
Email	aishaqchetty@hotmail.com
Nationality	British
Date of birth	30.05.1984

WORK EXPERIENCE

Dates	September 2003 to present
Employer	Western IT, 11 Randolph Road, Edinburgh, EH16 2NY, UK
Position held	Computing Support Officer
Main activities and responsibilities	Providing support in the field to a wide range of companies

EDUCATION AND TRAINING

Dates	September 2000 to August 2003
Organization	Simpson College, Glasgow, UK
Qualification	Higher National Diploma
Main subjects / skills covered	Computing (Technical support), Operating systems, Hardware installation and maintenance, Network building and maintenance

PERSONAL SKILLS AND COMPETENCES

Mother tongue	English – excellent communicator
Other languages	Good spoken French, some Hindi
Social skills	My work involves communicating with a wide range of clients with computing problems who often need help urgently. I work well under pressure.
Organizational skills	At college I organized a class visit to France Telecom.
Technical skills and competences	Familiar with most current operating systems, Novell, and Windows networks

ADDITIONAL INFORMATION

– Clean driving licence
– Personal interests include rock climbing and cycling

---

2 Make notes in order to write your own CV. You can invent work experience for this task.

The **number 1 rule** in preparing for a job interview is to research your target company *before* the interview. The **number 2 rule** in preparing for a job interview is to research the *competition* of your target company before the interview.
Carol Fillipino, *Recruitment Consultant*

Pairwork

1 Study the personality test designed to help you choose a suitable career.

1 What do you like doing?

2 What are you *good at* doing?

3 How do you see yourself? Choose adjectives from this list:

practical	ambitious
artistic	scientific
helpful	orderly

4 What do you value most in life?
practical things
science
creative arts
helping people
success

2 Work in pairs, A and B. Ask each other the questions in **1**. Decide which of these adjectives best describe your partner.

realistic	someone who would like to do practical work
social	someone who would like to work with people
investigative	someone who would like to do research
enterprising	someone who would like to start their own business
artistic	someone who is creative
conventional	someone who likes things as they are

3 Decide which of the jobs described in this book or listed on p.98 would suit your partner best.

4 When applying for a job, people often prepare a short personal statement to summarize their best qualities. Which of these expressions describe you?

creative	a good team player
dependable	like a challenge
energetic	motivated
experienced	skilled
hard-working	well-organized

5 Prepare a short personal statement about yourself. Be positive, but don't exaggerate your qualities! Read your statement to your partner and try to improve it together.

EXAMPLE

I'm a skilled technician who likes a challenge. I'm a dependable, energetic worker who is happy to work independently or as part of a team.

Pronunciation

Stress in long words (2)

1 🎧 Listen to these words from Units 10–14. Write the number of syllables in each word.

a computer	e microprocessor	i supercomputer
b co-operative	f petroleum	j telecommunications
c download	g prototype	k ultrasound
d hydraulic	h simulator	l vibrate

2 Put these words from Units 10–14 in columns 1–3 of the table according to their stress pattern.

animator	energetic	information
anticlockwise	enterprising	motivated
capacity	entertainment	peripheral
dependable	environment	simulation
development	indicator	ventilated

1 ●●●●	2 ●●●●●	3 ●●●●

3 🎧 Now listen and check your answers.

Speaking

Job interview

1 Work in pairs, A and B.

Student A Go to p.113.

Student B You are the applicant for the Stage Technician job (p.100).

List the questions you think the interviewer will ask. Prepare answers to them.

EXAMPLES

● *Which subjects did you enjoy most in your course?*
Think of reasons why you enjoyed particular subjects. Explain why your qualifications will be important.
● *What work experience do you have?*
Describe any part-time work, voluntary work, or work placement you have done.
● *Why do you want this job?*
Think of reasons why this job is important to you.
● *Why do you think you would be good at this job?*
Think about your qualifications, work experience, and interests.
Consider what kind of person you are. List your good points.
● *What do you do in your free time?*
List any sports or other interests.

Think of three questions to ask the interviewer.

EXAMPLES

● *Who would I work with?*
● *What training is there for the job?*

Now role-play the interview with Student A.

2 🎧 Listen to an extract from an interview for the Stage Technician job. Then change roles so that Student A is the applicant and Student B is the interviewer. Repeat your interview.

Key words

Adjectives
colour-blind
off-shore

Nouns
carpentry
competences
CV
experience
interview
lighting
maintenance
project management
recording studio
requirement
sound system
training

Verb
supervise

Note here anything about how English is used in technology that is **new** to you.

15 The future of technology

Switch on

Work in small groups. Discuss the predictions about technology. Decide which ones are most likely to happen and when they will happen.

1 Medical robots will carry out operations, controlled by surgeons who may be hundreds of kilometres away.

2 Tiny robots will be injected into our bodies to deliver medicine and to perform surgery from the inside.

3 You will be able to interact with characters in a TV programme and follow a storyline of your choice.

4 Planes will be controlled by computers which think like humans and are therefore afraid to crash.

5 Cars will be made of composites, plastic, and fibreglass, and will be assembled in six hours.

6 Cars will automatically drive at safe speeds and safe distances from each other.

7 You will be able to download your brain to a computer before you die.

8 Microchips will be stuck to your skin to form different circuits, including computers. You'll be able to watch a DVD using your arm as a screen.

9 Business will be carried out in 3-D virtual space, not in offices.

10 Active make-up will change to any shade you want.

11 Jobs like teaching children or nursing will continue to be done by people, but most other jobs will be done by robots and computers.

12 We'll be able to 'grow' plastics and fabrics from molecules.

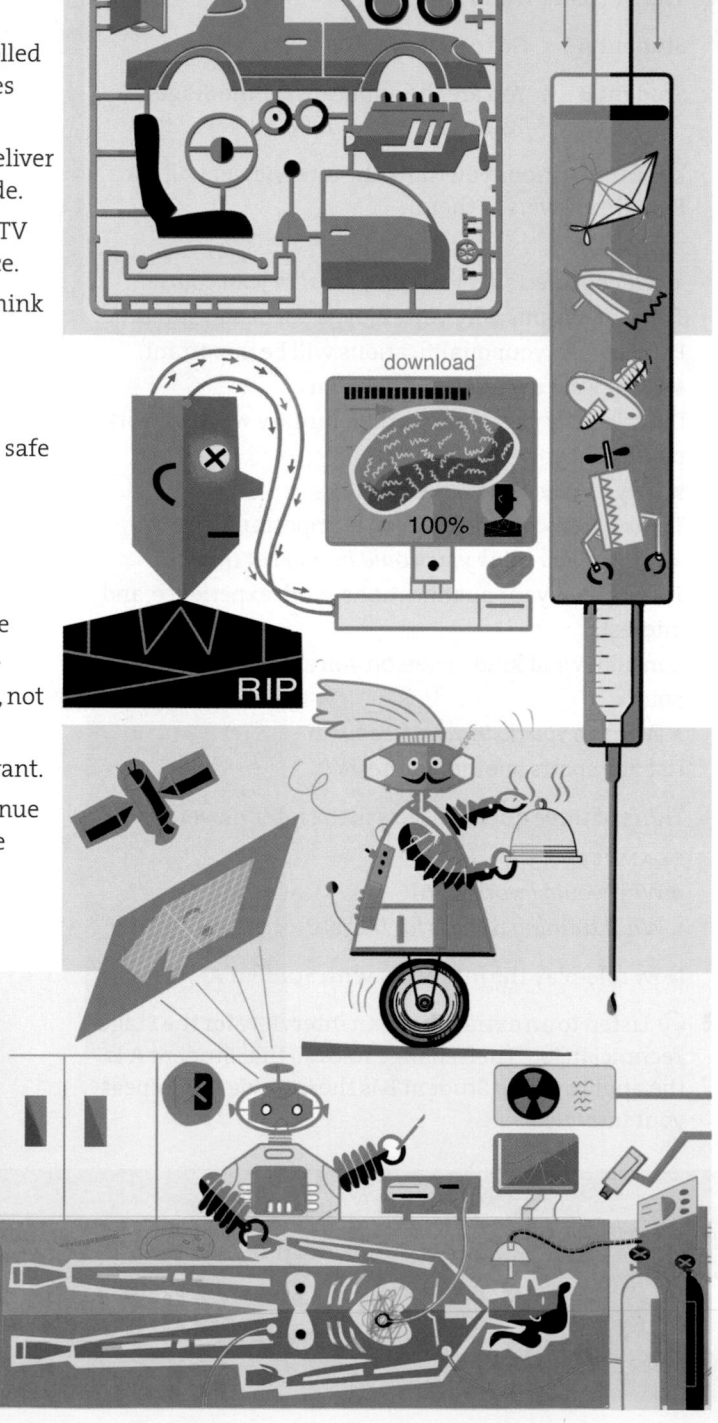

Listening
Predictions

1 🎧 Work in groups, A and B. Listen to this radio debate between two futurologists, Lianne Bradley and Stefan Werner. They are discussing technology in the future.

Group A Listen to Lianne's comments.

Group B Listen to Stefan's comments.

As you listen, tick (✓) the table to indicate which areas of technology the speaker mentions.

Lianne (Group A)	Stefan (Group B)	Prediction about
		1 transport
		2 health
		3 IT
		4 telecommunications
		5 military
		6 crime
		7 domestic
		8 developing countries

2 🎧 In the same groups, listen again and note down the predictions made by your speaker.

3 Now work with someone from the other group. Explain your speaker's predictions to each other. Decide together which predictions you accept.

● Language spot
Phrasal verbs

● Study these sentences:
*His father **set up** the company in 1965.*
*The company **closed down** in 2002.*
*Try to **work out** the answer.*

● The words in **bold** are phrasal verbs. Phrasal verbs consist of a verb + an adverb such as *down, off, on, out,* or *up*. Some of these words can also be used as prepositions.

● Many phrasal verbs have two meanings:
***Look up**, then look down.*	*(a doctor speaking)*
***Look up** any new words in a dictionary.*	*(a teacher speaking)*

>> Go to **Grammar reference** p.123

Study the phrasal verbs below. Put each one in the correct sentence.

carry out	give up	shut off
close down	plug in	switch off
cut down	print out	switch on
find out	set up	work out

1 In future, robots will _____ operations instead of humans.

2 Will we _____ cars and use public transport?

3 We'll be able to use the Web to _____ the answers to almost every question.

4 It's important that we _____ pollution in cities.

5 If you don't have a dictionary, you can often _____ the meaning of a new word from the words around it.

6 When you _____ the petrol engine, the electric motor starts running.

7 It's my job to _____ all the equipment before the concert begins.

8 Old industries will _____ but new industries will take their place.

9 The first step is to _____ and _____ the equipment.

10 Click 'Print' and select the number of copies to _____ .

11 To avoid electrical damage, always _____ the machine when it's not in use.

Gadget box

Mitsubishi have developed a robot, called Wakamaru, which can identify up to ten people and talk to them. It can recognize 10,000 words. It will wake you up in the morning and remind you of all the things you have to do that day. If you go on holiday, you can leave it to look after your house. It will report any problems by mobile phone.

What household tasks would you most like a robot to perform for you?

Pronunciation

Linking in phrasal verbs

Phrasal verbs are sometimes difficult to understand because of linking.

1 🎧 Listen to these examples.
Set it up.
Cut them off.

2 🎧 Listen and mark the linking in examples 1–10.

1	Line them up.	6	Shut it down.
2	Give it up.	7	Start it up.
3	Work it out.	8	Print them out.
4	Switch it off.	9	Plug it in.
5	Find it out.	10	Turn it on.

3 Work in pairs and say sentences 1–8. Time each other and see who can say them fastest without making a mistake.

1 Don't switch it on, switch it off.
2 Start it up when he's plugged it in.
3 Take it out to see if it turns on, then turn it over.
4 Find it out before they find it out and we'll get ahead.
5 Print them out so you can line them up and see the difference.
6 Shut it down now, not later – if you do it later, it's too late to start it up.
7 Turn it up by turning 'Up' and turn it down by turning 'Down' – it's simple!
8 If we work it out today, we won't have to find it out before we set it up tomorrow.

4 Write some phrasal verb 'tongue-twisters' of your own and practise saying them with a partner.

Pairwork

Work in pairs, A and B. Each of you has information about a future development in technology. Take notes from your text so that you can explain the main points to your partner without looking at the text. Listen carefully to your partner so you can summarize their text.

Student A   Go to p.113.

Student B

INKJET TECHNOLOGY

A new use has been found for an old technology. Inkjet printers are being developed which can place tiny amounts of ink precisely in the right place. Using metal inks containing very small particles of copper or silver, this technology can be used to make printed circuits. It can also be used to print electronic components including semiconductors and even batteries.

The technology has much wider applications. In future it may be used to print support structures which contain human cells. These will be used to help the body grow new skin, bone, or even organs. It will be possible to print pills, insect traps, and even wallpaper which contains its own lighting.

The telephone is a wonderful invention. I can foresee the day when there will be one in every city.
Unknown, circa 1890

Vocabulary

Affixes

1 Some technical words in English begin or end with common affixes. Knowing the meaning of the affix can help you work out the meaning of the whole word. Study the examples below.

Affix	Meaning	Example
bio	life	biotechnology
ex	out of	external
inter	between	Internet
intra	inside, within	intranet
less	without	wireless
micro	very small	microwave
mini	small	minidisk
poly	many	polyester
pre	before, earlier	prefabricated
super	above, much greater	supermarket
tele	far, distant	telecommunications

2 Using the table, work out the words which have the following meanings.

1 medicine at a distance
2 a very small electronic chip
3 a plastic containing many molecules of carbon
4 an instrument for measuring very small thicknesses
5 concrete which has been stressed earlier
6 a computer much more powerful than ordinary computers
7 a very small processor
8 a fan which removes air and blows it out
9 a phone without a cord
10 measuring according to biological data

Customer care

Saying goodbye

How many of these informal ways of saying goodbye do you know? Do they have equivalents in your language?

Quiz

Work in groups of three. One student is the quizmaster and asks the questions for part A. The other two students work individually and write their answers. Change roles for parts B and C. Then find out who has remembered the most!

A (Units 1–5)

1 Give a negative and a positive effect of technology on society.
2 What are the comparative forms of *fast* and *efficiently*?
3 Name one of the ways that the Airbus 380 is larger than the Boeing 747.
4 What does *ABS* stand for?
5 Which part of the word *engineer* is stressed?
6 Name one course civil engineering students take.
7 Correct this sentence: *I'm liking calculus*.
8 Complete this sentence: *Electrical engineering is about …*
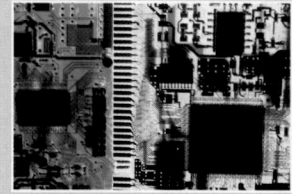
9 Which branch of technology does this picture represent?
10 What is *Autocad*?
11 Name one of the stages in the design process.
12 Which word means 'the first example of a new type of design'?
13 Name a famous designer.
14 In design, what is the *brief*?
15 Make a question to get this answer: *Because it's easy to mould*.
16 Name two materials used for bike frames.
17 What property describes the capacity of a material to stretch?
18 *Strong* is an adjective. What is the noun?
19 Name something in the world of sport made of *lycra*.
20 What is a *laminate*?
21 Which verb goes with *spring*?
22 Which verb describes two gears making contact?
23 Name one of the strokes of a two-stroke engine.
24 Write down this number in words: 10^{-12}
25 What is the adjective which describes a movement from side to side like a pendulum?

B (Units 6–10)

1 Name an item of police equipment.
2 What item of equipment do police use to restrain someone?
3 What does *PIN* stand for?
4 What do you call a seal which air can't pass through?
5 What can a *smart gun* do?
6 What are most drinks cans made of?
7 Fill the gap: *Loaves are taken out of their tins _____ suction*.
8 What process is used to make CD covers?
9 What material is used to make soft drinks cans?
10 Fill the gap: *A clockwork radio is a radio _____ clockwork*.
11 What does *ASV* stand for?
12 What do we call a car with a petrol engine and an electric motor?
13 Name a disadvantage of electric cars.
14 What word do we use to describe 'very heavy traffic that slows down movement on the roads'?
15 If you tell a customer that you *very much regret* something, what are you doing?
16 What do we call the outer walls of a skyscraper?
17 Fill the gap: *All exposed metalwork is _____ in case of fire*.
18 If something is *flammable* what can it do?
19 What does this sign mean?

20 Which part of the word *automatic* is normally stressed?
21 Why does an artificial heart have *two* batteries?
22 What kind of switch works by air pressure?
23 Complete this sentence: *A pacemaker is a device …*
24 What kind of signals does the Ultracane transmit?
25 What is the opposite of *forwards*?

Checklist

Assess your progress in this unit.
Tick (✓) the statements which are true.

- ☐ I can discuss predictions about technology
- ☐ I know how to use common phrasal verbs
- ☐ I know how to link phrasal verbs when speaking
- ☐ My reading and listening are good enough to understand most of each text in this unit

Key words

Adverb
automatically

Adjectives
blurred (vision)
smart
stressed
unmanned
virtual
voice-operated

Nouns
chip
intranet
prediction
processor
virus

Verbs
interact
report
stick

Note here anything about how English is used in technology that is **new** to you.

C (Units 11–15)

1 What does *CGI* stand for?
2 What is *demo* short for?
3 What verb do we use to describe copying tracks to CDs from online sites?
4 Fill the gap: *You _____ touch a flat screen. It's easy to damage it.*
5 What do we call a person who plays games to find faults?
6 What does *CIM* stand for?
7 What verb do we use to describe how a computer can make something, like a car crash, seem real?
8 Fill the gap: *In the past, designs _____ produced on paper.*
9 How is the -ed ending pronounced in *finished*: /t/, /d/, or /ɪd/?
10 Cross out the silent letter in the word *pneumatic*.
11 Name two devices used in telecommunications.
12 Put the verb in brackets in the correct form: *I (be) with this company for 5 years. I like it here.*
13 Fill the gap: *VoIP phones send data over the Internet in tiny packets. This is called _____ .*
14 What does *LCD* stand for?
15 When did email start (±5 years)?
16 What do we call an engineer who is concerned with buildings and other structures?
17 Name one thing that a Sound Engineer does.
18 Fill the gap: *Anyone who works with electrical wiring _____ be colour-blind.*
19 What do we call a document which lists all your work experience and qualifications?
20 What do we call a person or organization which gives you work?
21 Fill the gap: *When we say what will happen in the future, we make a _____ .*
22 What is the correct phrasal verb? *His father set down / on / up the company in 1994.*
23 Fill the gap: *Drivers should _____ up their cars and use public transport instead.*
24 What do we call a computer network within a company or organization?
25 What does *micro* mean?

Pairwork activities

Unit 1 p.8

Student A

	Student A's launch system	Student B's launch system
	Ariane 5	Proton M
Country	European Space Agency	
First launched	1996	
Height	51m	
Diameter	5.4m	
Engines	6	
Payload GTO (geostationary transfer orbit)	6,800 kg	
Mass	230,000 kg	
Lift-off thrust	6,360 kN	

Unit 2 p.13

Student A

	09.00–11.00	11.15–13.00	14.00–15.30	15.30–16.30
Mon	SELF-STUDY			
Tues	_____ R110	Hardware installation & maintenance R110	_____	Client operating systems R102
Wed	Computer operating systems R105	_____ R107	Free	Free
Thur	_____ _____	Program planning A104	_____ A104	Free
Fri	Networks R105	Communication skills T105	Free	Free

Unit 3 p.21

Student A

James Dyson (1947–) UK engineer, inventor, and multi-millionaire who has developed a range of very popular 'bagless' domestic vacuum cleaners and other products.

Unit 4 p.26

Student A

Skateboard

Part/Component	Materials used	Reason

Snowboard

Snowboards are made from wood and laminated fibre-glass. Wood is used for the core. The combination of wood and fibreglass gives the board strength with little weight. It also makes the board flexible. The base of the board is covered with *p-tex*, a kind of tough plastic which helps the board slide but resists wear. It has a curved steel edge which helps the board to grip the snow. Bindings, made of nylon, are fixed to the top of the snowboard.

Unit 12 p.91
Student A

Unit 5 p.31
Student A

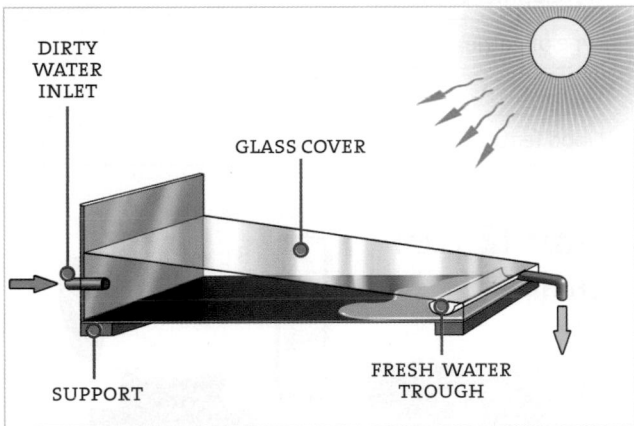

Unit 5 p.33
Student A

You are a technician at a **plant** hire company. You have two possible generators for the customer to **hire** (Model A and Model B). Help the customer to make the right choice. Check what domestic appliances the customer has. Remind the customer that he / she may not need to run the generator all night. A typical home uses 2.4 kW for lighting. With all major appliances on at the same time, this rises to 6.6 kW.

Useful language
What electric appliances do you have at home?
Do you need to run the generator all night?

	Model A	Model B
output	4.5 kW	8 kW
voltage	120 or 240 AC	120 or 240 AC
fuel	diesel	diesel
running time before refuelling	8 hours	24 hours
noise level	enclosed motor (88 dB)	fully sound-proofed (60 dB)
starting	electric starter	electric starter
cost per day	€25	€70
delivery charge	€20	€30

Unit 6 p.36
Student A

Smart gun recognizes its owner

The New Jersey Institute of Technology has developed a new system for hand guns called dynamic grip recognition. Sensors are fitted into the handle of the gun and trained to recognize only the owner's grip. Hand grips, like fingerprints and iris patterns, are unique. The sensors read the pressure of the grip in the first second the trigger is pressed. If it doesn't match the owner's grip, the gun will refuse to fire.

The inventors say it will prevent incidents where police have been shot with their own guns or where children have been killed playing with a parent's gun. Early results from trials with New Jersey police show the system works.

Unit 7 p.43
Student A

A
Next, the glass master is placed into an electrolytic solution containing a silver rod. Current is applied and a thin layer of silver forms over the glass face. The process is called electroforming. It produces a rigid metal negative to the master, which is called the Father.

B

The digital signal to be recorded is sent to a laser. The laser is aimed at a spinning glass disc coated with a photoresist chemical. As the laser turns on and off, the resist is burnt off or remains, matching the exact pattern of the signal.

C

The stampers are placed in a moulding press. Melted plastic is injected into the moulds and allowed to cool. This produces a clear plastic disc, a substrate, with the pits of the original recording accurately copied on one side.

Unit 9 p.72

Student A

Friction pile

Reinforced concrete piles which are used in soft soil which becomes stiffer with depth. The piles stay in place because of the squeezing force of the soil round them.

Floating raft

A raft of reinforced concrete. For situations when the ground is soft or there are tunnels or mines under the ground which could cause collapse.

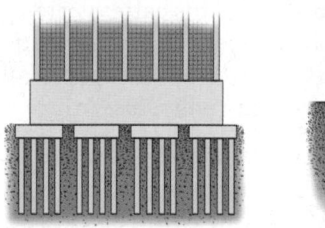 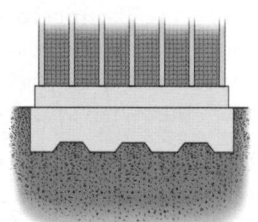

Unit 10 p.79

Student A

Device	a) What it's for	b) How it works
Bed occupancy sensor		
Carbon monoxide detector (wireless)		
Floor detector		
Gas shut-off valve		
Medication dispenser		
Property exit sensor		

Unit 11 p.85

Student A

Jade Empire

This is a role-playing game. You play the part of a student at a martial arts school. Your village is attacked. You get to explore imaginary worlds and fight with enemies. It was developed by BioWare for Microsoft. It's played on an Xbox. The real-time combat features are particularly good.

Name of the game	
Company / Development team	
Type of game	
Console	
Good features	

Unit 12 p.91

Student B

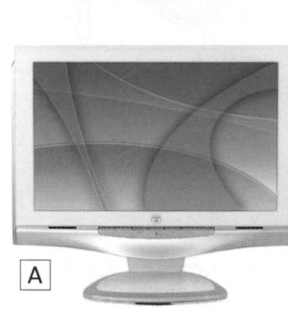 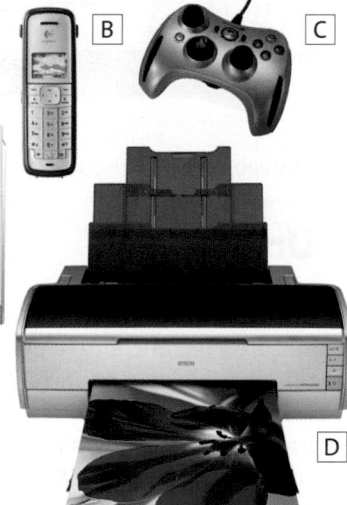

Unit 5 p.31
Student B

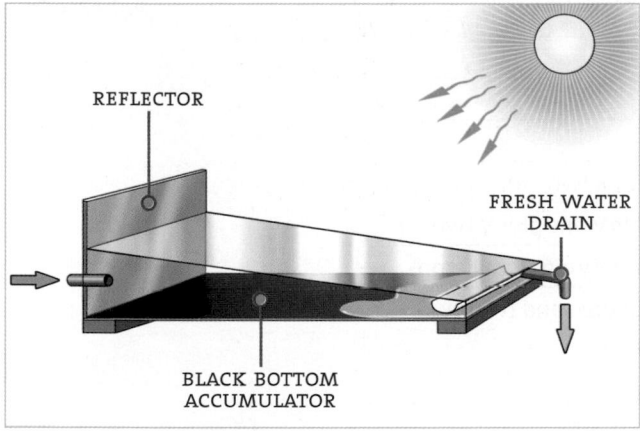

Unit 13 p.94
Student A

	A	B
Make	Motorola	
Model	RAZR	
Keyboard type	full Qwerty	
Screen	320 x 240 pixel, 65K thin film transistor, liquid crystal display	
Software	Microsoft Pocket Explorer, Outlook, Word, Windows Media	
Other features	1.3 megapixel camera	
	Bluetooth	
	MP3, AAC, WMA and WAV audio file playback and video capture	
Email	compatible with a variety of services	

Unit 14 p.103
Student A

You are the interviewer for the job of Stage Technician (p.100). Write a list of questions to ask the applicant.

EXAMPLES
- *What work experience have you had?*
- *Why do you want this job?*
- *Why do you think you would be good at this job?*
- *What are your strengths?*
- *Describe a difficult situation you handled well.*

Give the candidate a chance to ask you questions about the job.

Unit 15 p.106
Student A

E INK

In the past, flickering screens made electronic books and newspapers uncomfortable to read for long periods. The American company, E Ink, has solved this problem by producing electronic ink. The system works by forming thousands of black and white capsules into letters which are almost as good as printed characters. They appear on screens which are as thin as paper and can be bent without causing damage.

Different companies have released products which use this new technology. Seiko has produced a watch which you can bend round your wrist. Sony has released its Reader device. It is no thicker than a paperback and weighs just 250 grammes. It has a six-inch screen and can store books and comic books downloaded from the Internet. It accepts both memory sticks and SD flash memory cards. Sony claims the batteries will allow up to 7,500 page turns.

On the downside, it has no backlight and with comic books the batteries can be exhausted in twenty hours.

Symbols and characters

Mathematical symbols

SYMBOL	EXAMPLE	READ AS
.	8.5689	eight *point* five six eight nine
+	$R_1 + R_2$	R one *plus* R two
−	$V - V_1$	V *minus* V one
±	±3m	*plus or minus* 3 metres
=	$R = R_1 + R_2$	R *equals / is equal to* R one plus R two
≠	$V \neq V_1 + V_2$	V *doesn't equal / is not equal to* V one plus V two
≈ or ≃	I ≈ 28 mA	I is *approximately equal to* twenty eight milliamps
×	f ×120	f *times / multiplied by* one hundred and twenty
no sign between two quantities	E = IR	E *equals* I *times / multiplied by* R
one quantity over another	$\dfrac{I}{R}$	I *over / divided by* R / *The ratio of* I *to* R
÷	36 ÷ 5 =7.2	thirty six *divided by* five equals seven point two
∝	I ∝ V	I *is proportional to* V
:	11:1	*(a ratio of)* eleven *to* one
%	25%	twenty-five *per cent*
°	30°C	thirty *degrees* celsius
√	√5	*the square root of / root of* five
2	R^2	R *squared*
3	X^3	X *cubed*
4	10^4	ten *to the power four*
-8	10^{-8}	ten *to the power minus eight*
>	>10 dB	*greater than* ten decibels
<	<25 mA	*less than* twenty-five milliamps
≥	≥5W	*greater than or equal to* five watts
≤	≤10W	*less than or equal to* ten watts

url characters

SYMBOL	READ AS	EXAMPLES
/	forward slash	www.tinyurl.com/qat7n
\	back slash	w w w dot tiny u r l dot com forward slash q a t 7 n
.	dot	http://www.mercedes-benz.com
:	colon	h t t p colon double forward slash w w w dot mercedes hyphen benz dot com
-	hyphen	
–	underscore	

Grammar reference

1 Comparisons with adjectives and adverbs

Comparative adjectives

		Adjective	Comparative
one-syllable adjectives	add -*er*	*fast*	*faster*
one-syllable adjectives ending in -*e*	add -*r*	*safe*	*safer*
two-syllable adjectives ending in -*y*	change -*y* to -*ier*	*easy*	*easier*
adjectives with two or more syllables	*more* + adjective	*realistic*	*more realistic*
irregular adjectives		*good* *bad* *far*	*better* *worse* *farther / further*

*Computers are **faster** today.*
*This report is **more realistic**.*

When we compare two things or situations directly, we use the comparative + *than*.

*The programs today are **more sophisticated than** in the past.*
NOT *The programs today are* ~~more sophisticated that~~ *in the past.*

Comparative adverbs

		Adverb	Comparative
adverbs with same form as adjectives	add -*er*	*fast*	*faster*
	add -*r*	*late*	*later*
	change -*y* to -*ier*	*early*	*earlier*
adverbs ending in -*ly*	*more* + adverb	*slowly*	*more slowly*
irregular adverbs		*good* *bad* *far*	*well* *worse* *farther / further*

We can use *less* with adjectives and adverbs of two or more syllables to mean the opposite of *more*.

*Computers were **less powerful** in the past.*
*They worked **less efficiently**.*

We can add *much* before comparative adjectives and adverbs to suggest a stronger comparison.

*These sales figures are **much worse** than I expected.*
*That report was written **much more recently** than this one.*

2 Present Simple v Present Continuous

Present Simple

Positive

I / You / We / They	enjoy maths.
He / She / It	enjoys maths.

= subject + verb

Negative

I / You / We / They	**don't** want to be an engineer.
He / She / It	**doesn't** want to be an engineer.

= subject + *do / does* + *not* + infinitive

Questions		Short answers
Do I / you / we / they	like the proposal?	Yes, I / you / we / they **do**.
Does he / she / it	like the proposal?	Yes, he / she / it **does**.
		No, I / you / we / they **don't**.
		No, he / she / it **doesn't**.

= *Do / Does* + subject + infinitive

Note that in short answers we use the full forms *do / does* in positive responses, and the short forms *don't / doesn't* in negative responses.

We use the Present Simple to talk about
- things that are always true
- repeated actions
- verbs that describe thinking and feeling.

*Water **boils** at 100°C.*
*She **doesn't go** to college on Fridays.*
***Do** you **think** the amount of traffic will increase?*

Present Continuous

Positive

I	**am** study**ing**	to be an engineer.
You / We / They	**are** study**ing**	to be an engineer.
He / She / It	**is** study**ing**	to be an engineer.

= subject + **am** / **are** / **is** + **-ing** form

Negative

I	**'m not**	start**ing**	the course until September.
You / We / They	**aren't**	start**ing**	the course until September.
He / She / It	**isn't**	start**ing**	the course until September.

= subject + **am** / **are** / **is** + **not** + **-ing** form

Questions

Questions			Short answers
Am	I	work**ing** on this project?	Yes, I **am**.
Are	you / we / they	work**ing** on this project?	Yes, you / we / they **are**.
Is	he / she / it	work**ing** on this project?	Yes, he / she / it **is**.
			No, I**'m not**.
			No, you / we / they **aren't**.
			No, he / she / it **isn't**.

= **Am** / **are** / **is** + subject + **-ing** form

Note: In short answers we use the full forms *am* / *is* / *are* in positive responses, and the short forms *'m not* / *aren't* / *isn't* in negative responses.

We use the Present Continuous to talk about
● things that are happening now
● things that are happening for a limited period of time around now.

She's working at the Telford office today.
I'm studying to be a surveyor.

Remember that we can use most verbs in both the Present Simple and the Present Continuous, except the verbs of thinking and feeling such as *know, want, feel, think, like*.

With the Present Continuous, we often use a time expression such as *now, currently, at the moment, this year*.

With the Present Simple, we can use expressions that refer to a specific point in time, such as *on Tuesday, at nine o'clock*

or adverbs and expressions of frequency such as *usually, always, on Wednesdays, three days a week*.

3 Question types

There are two main types of questions. Those which require a *Yes / No* answer, and information or *Wh-* questions, which ask for specific information.

Yes / No questions

These begin with an auxiliary verb, such as *do, am / is / are, have / has, can, could, will, must*, etc.

Positive

Positive			Short answers
Have	you	finished the prototype?	Yes, I **have**.
Does	the prototype	work?	Yes, it **does**.
Will	the designs	be ready in time?	Yes, they will.

= auxiliary verb + subject + main verb (+ object)

Negative

Negative			
Haven't	you	finished the prototype?	No, I **haven't**.
Doesn't	the prototype	work?	No, it **doesn't**.
Won't	the designs	be ready in time?	No, they **won't**.

= auxiliary verb + **not** + subject + main verb (+ object)

Information questions

These begin with question words, such as *what, who, when, where, why, which*, and *how*. We can use *how* in other combinations, such as *how much, how many, how long, how far, how safe*, etc.

The question words *what, which, how much*, and *how many* can be followed by a noun.

What	do	you		think of this solution?
How many	machines	has	the company	bought?

= question word (+ object) + auxiliary + subject + main verb

In the two sentences above, the question word is the object of the main verb. Note that *what, who, which, how much, how many* can also be the subject of a question. In this case, the word order is the same as in a positive sentence.

Which	solution	works best?
How many	*machines*	*are in here?*
Who		*designed the prototype?*

= question word (+ subject) + main verb

4 *used to, used for, made of, made from*

We use *used to* and *used for* to describe how materials are used. We use *made of* and *made from* to talk about the materials that a product consists of.

used to

Rubber **is used to** make the pedals.

= subject + *is / are used to* + infinitive

used for

Leather **is used for** making footballs.

= *is / are used for* + -ing form

We can use **used to** and **used for** in a similar way.
*Nylon **is used to** make / **used for** making a lot of different products.*

Note: Don't confuse these expressions with *be used to* + -ing form, which means 'be accustomed to'.

made of

Some bottles **are made of** plastic.

= subject + *is / are made of* + noun

made from

Steel **is made from** iron and carbon.

= subject + *is / are made from* + noun

Made from emphasizes the result of a process, while

made of simply lists the materials that a product consists of. However, in practice, these expressions are often used to have the same meaning.
*Some bottles are **made of** / **made from** plastic.*
*Steel is **made of** / **made from** iron and carbon.*

5 Time clauses

We use *when, as, before, after* to show clearly the order in which different events happened. The part of the sentence that begins with the time expression is called the 'time clause'.

when

We use *when* to refer to actions that happen at almost the same time. One action is an immediate consequence of another. Note that when the time clause comes first, it must be followed by a comma.
***When** you turn the handle, the wheel starts to move.*

We can change the two parts of the sentence around, but *when* must always come before the first action in the sequence of events.
*The wheel starts to move **when you turn the handle**.*

When the time clause comes later in the sentence, we do not use a comma to separate the two clauses.

as

We use *as* to talk about two actions that happen at the same time. The position of the time clause can change, in the same way as for *when*.
***As** the wheel turns, it generates electricity.*
*The wheel generates electricity **as** it turns.*

Note that in the second *as* sentence, we need to use a subject *the wheel*, because by changing the order of the clauses, it is no longer clear what *it* refers to.

before and *after*

Before and *after* also indicate the sequence of events, but there is not necessarily such a close time relationship as with *when* and *as*. *Before* and *after* simply indicate that one action happened at an unspecified time before another.

Again, the position of the time clause can change.
***Before** you operate the machine, you must read the manual.*
*You must read the manual **before** you operate the machine.*

*Trevor Baylis developed his clockwork radio **after** he visited Africa.*
***After** he visited Africa, Trevor Baylis developed his clockwork radio.*

Before and *after* can be followed by the *-ing* form instead of subject + verb.

***Before** operating the machine, you must read the manual.*
***After** visiting Africa, Trevor Baylis developed his clockwork radio.*

6 Describing function

We use *used to, (used) for, used as* to describe the function of an object in positive and negative sentences, and in questions.

used to + infinitive

*A torch is **used to** provide light.*
*Tasers aren't **used to** protect computers.*
*Is a baton **used to** monitor criminals?*

(used) for + *-ing* form

This expression has the same meaning as *be used to* + infinitive.

*Handcuffs are **(used) for** restraining someone.*
*The baton isn't **(used) for** monitoring criminals.*
*Is a PIN **(used) for** protecting cards?*

Note that although we can leave out *used* in *be used for*, we cannot leave out *used* in the expression *be used to*.

Note: Don't confuse these expressions with *be used to* + *-ing* form, which means 'be accustomed to'.

used as + noun

This expression also describes the purpose of an object, to show that it is similar to the function of another object.

*The belt **is used as** a weapon.*
*The handcuffs **aren't used as** a weapon.*
*Is the torch **used as** a signal?*

We cannot use this expression if the two objects have exactly the same function.

NOT *A torch is used as a light.*

7 Present Passive

One way to describe processes is to use the Present Simple.

*The plastic **travels** through the barrel.*
*The mould **is** now cool.*

However, it is more common to use the Passive. This is because, when talking about a process, it is often not important or relevant to mention who performs an action.

Some verbs, such as verbs which do not take an object, e.g. *travel*, or verbs of thinking and feeling, e.g. *be*, cannot usually be used in the Passive.

NOT *The plastic is travelled through the barrel.*

Present Passive

Positive

The dough	**is cut**	into loaves.
The loaves	**are left**	to cool.

= subject + *am / is / are* + past participle

Negative

The plastic	**isn't melted**	by the hydraulic fluid.
The screws	**aren't pushed**	back by the ram.

= subject + *am / is / are not* + past participle

Questions				Short answers
Is	the hopper	**filled**	with plastic?	Yes, it **is**. No, it **isn't**.
Are	the loaves	**sent**	to the shops?	Yes, they **are**. No, they **aren't**.

= *Am / Is / Are* + subject + past participle

How is the plastic **melted**?

= Question word + *am / is / are* + subject + past participle

Although in general contexts the Passive can have *I / you / we* as the subject, when talking about processes the subject is generally the pronoun *it* or *they*, or a singular or plural noun.

Note: The Passive can be followed with *by* if we need to clarify who or what has caused the action.

8 Prediction: *will, may, might*

will

We use *will* to talk about future developments that we are certain about.

Positive

One sensor	**will**	stop	the driver falling asleep.

= subject + *will* + infinitive

Negative

Traffic congestion	**will not** be		an easy problem to solve.

= subject + *will not (won't)* + infinitive

Questions

How **will**	the car of the future	be powered?
Will	the car of the future	be very different?

= (question word +) *will* + subject + infinitive

may and *might*

We use *may* and *might* when we are less certain about future developments, i.e. when we think that something is possible rather than definite. *May* is more formal than *might*, but there is little difference in the level of possibility they contain.

Positive

A hybrid car	**may / might**	be the best choice.

= subject + *may / might* + infinitive

Negative

A noise-free bike	**may not / might not**	be popular with bikers.

= subject + *may / might* + *not* + infinitive

Questions

Might	hydrogen fuel cells	get cheaper?

= *Might* + subject + infinitive

How **might**	the car of the future	be powered?

= question word + *might* + subject + infinitive

We can use the short form *mightn't* in spoken English, but there is no short form for *may not*.
Traffic congestion mightn't be an easy problem to solve.

NOT *Traffic congestion ~~mayn't~~ be an easy problem to solve.*

May is not used when we are asking people for their opinions, in order to avoid confusion with *may* in requests.

9 Safety signs and safety advice

There are several ways of giving instructions and advice in safety signs and notices.

No + *-ing* or noun

This is a direct command to the public, and is found on signs in a range of general and industrial contexts.
No smoking
No admittance

Imperative

This type of command is not as strict as *no + -ing*, and can be found in more informal signs, or in safety handbooks.

Positive

Wear	a safety helmet.

= infinitive

Negative

Do not smoke	here.

= *Do not* + infinitive

The short form of *Do not* is *Don't*. This is used commonly in spoken English and in more informal advice or commands.
Don't keep your mobile phone switched on.

We can use *always* and *never* to make a command stronger. In a positive command, *always* comes just before the verb.
Always check the filters.

In a negative sentence, *never* replaces *do not / don't*.
Never operate the chainsaw without ear protection.

must

Must expresses a strong obligation and authority, and is used in both the Active and Passive. Remember that *must* does not change in the *he / she / it* forms.

Active form

You	**must**	wear a safety helmet.
Unauthorized persons	**must not**	use this machine.

= subject + **must (not)** + infinitive

Passive form

Eye protection	**must**	be worn.
Fire extinguishers	**must not**	be used in this area.

= subject + **must (not)** + **be** + past participle

We can also use *always* and *never* with *must*. In both the Active and Passive, *always* and *never* follow *must*.

*You must **always** wear a hard hat when work is going on overhead.*
*Personnel must **never** leave this equipment switched on.*
*High visibility clothing must **always** be worn in this area.*
*Chemicals must **never** be stored near open flames.*

10 Relative clauses

We use a relative clause as a means of joining two pieces of information together within one sentence.

The Ultracane is a device.
This device helps blind people.

Relative clause: *The Ultracane is **a device which** helps blind people.*

A cardiac patient is a person.
The person is being treated for a heart problem.

Relative clause: *A cardiac patient is **a person who** is being treated for a heart problem.*

In relative clauses, we use the relative pronouns *who* when the subject is a person, or *which* when the subject is an object.

Note that the subject of *who* and *which* can be singular or plural.
Ultracanes are devices which help blind people.
Cardiac patients are people who are being treated for heart problems.

There are two types of relative clause: defining and non-defining.

Defining relative clause

This tells us information about an object or person that identifies them.

This is a scanner which reads books. (= there are several types of scanner, and this is one that reads books)
There's the lab technician who works in the laboratory with me. (= there are several lab technicians, and he / she is the one who works with me)

Non-defining relative clause

This tells us supplementary information about an object or person. The relative pronoun *who* or *which* is always preceded by a comma.

This is a scanner, which reads books. (= there is only one type of scanner, and it happens to read books)
There's the lab technician, who works in the laboratory with me. (= there is only one lab technician, and he / she works with me)

11 should / shouldn't

We use *should* and *should not (shouldn't)* to give advice and to offer an opinion.

Positive

You	**should**	keep your password safe.

= subject + **should** + infinitive

Negative

People	**shouldn't**	download illegally.

= subject + **should** + **not (shouldn't)** + infinitive

Questions	Short answers
Should I update my virus protection software every month?	Yes, I / you / he / she / it / they **should**. No, I / you / he / she / it / they **shouldn't**.

= **Should** + subject + infinitive

What **should** I do?

Who **should** I complain to?

= question word + **should** + subject + infinitive

We do not use the auxiliary *do* / *does* to form the negative and questions.

NOT *They ~~don't should~~ download illegally* ...

NOT *~~Do I should~~* ...?

When we use *should* to give an opinion, we use *I think* / *I don't think* + subject + *should*.

I think you should buy the camera with 4 megapixels.
I don't think children should play violent video games.

In the second sentence above, it is also possible to say *I think* + subject + *shouldn't*:

I think children shouldn't play violent video games.

but this form is not as common as the first sentence.

12 Past Passive

We use the Past Passive to talk about systems and processes in the past. As with the Present Passive (Unit 7), we use the Past Passive when the action is more important than the agent, or where the agent is not known.

Positive

Welding	**was done**	by hand.

= subject + *was* / *were* + past participle

Negative

Cars	**were not (weren't) inspected**	by robots.

= subject + *was* / *were not (wasn't* / *weren't)* + past participle

Questions	Short answers
Were designs **produced** on computer?	Yes, they **were.** No, they **weren't.**

= *Was* / *Were* + subject + past participle

How **were** designs **produced**?

= question word + *was* / *were* + subject + past participle

We can use *by* after a Passive form to say who or what caused the action in a process.

*Supplies were ordered **by** staff, not **by** computer.*

13 Past Simple v Present Perfect

Past Simple

Positive

I / You / He / She / It / We / They	**texted**	her an invitation.

= subject + Past Simple

Negative

I/ You / He / She / It / We / They	**didn't work**	in Signals.

= subject + *did not (didn't)* + infinitive

Questions	Short answers
Did you work mainly indoors?	Yes, I / he / she / it / we / they **did.** No, I / he / she / it / we / they **didn't.**

= *Did* + subject + infinitive

● We use the Past Simple to talk about an action that happened at a particular point in the past.

*I **operated** different types of equipment.* (= it is clear that this person no longer operates different types of equipment)

● With the Past Simple we can use expressions such as *in* + year / month / season, *before*, and *after*.

Present Perfect

Positive

I	**have seen**	many changes in telecommunications.

= subject + *have* / *has* + past participle

Negative

She	**hasn't emailed**	me today.

= subject + *have* / *has not (haven't* / *hasn't)* + past participle

Questions

Have you **spent** time in the army?	Yes, I / you / we / they **have.** Yes, he / she / it **has.** No, I / you / we / they **haven't**. No, he / she / it **hasn't.**

= *Have / Has* + subject + **past participle**

We use the Present Perfect to talk about actions or experiences that happened during a period of time from the past to the present. It is not important when they occurred.

I've operated different types of equipment. (= at some point in this person's life, they have operated different types of equipment, and possibly still do)

We can begin talking about a topic in the Present Perfect, then use the Past Simple to add details about when something happened.

I've worked in Signals since 2003. Before that, I was a mechanic.

for / since

We can use both the Past Simple and the Present Perfect with *for*, and the Present Perfect with *since* to answer the question *How long?*

for + period of time, to say how long a period of time lasted: *for eight months, for two hours*
since + point in time to say when a period of time started: *since 2 o'clock, since 1993, since yesterday*

Present Perfect: *I've been here for a few months.*
Past Simple: *I was in the army for four years.*
Present Perfect: *I've worked here since I was eighteen.*

14 Job requirements

In addition to the functions of giving instructions (Unit 9) and advice (Unit 11), we can use *must* and *should* to describe essential characteristics that are necessary for a job or role.

must

Positive

Candidates	**must**	speak French and German.

= subject + *must* + infinitive

Negative

Applicants	**mustn't**	have less than three years' experience.

= subject + *must not (mustn't)* + infinitive

Here, *mustn't* = it is a requirement of the job that candidates do not have less than three years' experience. Do not confuse this with *don't have to* + infinitive, which means that something isn't necessary.

Questions	Short answers
Must candidates be British nationals?	Yes, I / you / he / she / it / they **must**.
	No, I / you / we / they **don't have to**.
	No, he / she / it **doesn't have to**.

= *Must* + subject + infinitive

Note that in negative short answers, we say *don't have to* rather than *mustn't*, because we want to say that something isn't necessary.

should

Positive

You	**should**	have experience of working with this system.

= subject + *should* + infinitive

Negative

Applicants	**should not (shouldn't)**	have a hearing disability.

= subject + *should not (shouldn't)* + infinitive

Questions	Short answers
Should applicants have a knowledge of public health issues?	Yes, I / you / he / she / it / they **should**.
	No, I / you / we / they **don't have to**.
	No, he / she / it **doesn't have to**.

= *Must* + subject + infinitive

Note that the negative short answer is the same as for *must*. *Must* is generally stronger than *should*, and means that a requirement is essential rather than merely desirable.

15 **Phrasal verbs**

Phrasal verbs consist of a verb + adverb or preposition, such as *in, out, up, down, off, on*, which combine to form a single meaning. Phrasal verbs are used very frequently in both spoken and written English.

The meaning of the two words together is often different from the meaning of the words individually, for example *put off* = to postpone or to delay. Some phrasal verbs have more than one meaning:

carry out = to perform an action
carry out = to take away or to take outside

One verb can be combined with different adverbs or prepositions to make different phrasal verbs, e.g. *set off, set out, set up*.

When phrasal verbs have an object, the position of the object changes if it is a pronoun.

*Try to work out **the answer**.*
OR *Try to work **the answer** out.*
BUT *Try to work **it** out.*
NOT *Try to ~~work out it~~.*

Other verbs in this group include:
carry out, close down, cut down, fill in, find out, give up, look up, plug in, print out, put on, set up, shut off, switch on / off, take off, turn down / off, work out

However some phrasal verbs must put the object immediately after the phrasal verb, e.g.

*Look for **the information**.*
*Look for **it**.*
NOT *~~Look it for~~.*
NOT *~~Look the information for~~.*

Listening scripts

Unit 1

Listening – Technology and work

1

I can get patients' lab results – blood and biochemistry – through the Health Service intranet. No delays, no need to wait for paper copies. It's much faster.

2

My students can use the Internet to practise their German. They exchange emails with German students – half the time in English, half in German. It's more realistic. And I can use the Web to get up-to-date material in German. I have a satellite receiver at home so I can watch German TV and record programmes for use in class.

3

People pay with plastic. Now it's more cards than cash. It's safer because there's less money in the shop but I have to pay the card companies each time. And I don't get my money if someone uses a stolen card.

4

It's not good. My sales are much worse. Instead of buying CDs, people download individual tracks from the Internet.

Pronunciation – Word stress

1	machine	7	technician
2	machinery	8	technology
3	mechanics	9	electron
4	mechanic	10	electronics
5	mechanical	11	electrical
6	technical	12	electrician

Unit 2

Listening – The course – part 1

I=Interviewer, A=Alec

I You're doing an HND in Civil engineering. How long does that last?
A It's a two-year course.
I And what stage are you at now?
A I'm in the second semester of the first year.
I How many students are in the group?
A There are eight, all men.

I Why did you decide to do this course?
A I left school at seventeen and started off as an Architectural Technician and …
I What did that involve, being an Architectural Technician?
A Doing all the technical drawings for the architects, things like that. We used a program called Autocad.
I And what took you into that line of business?
A Well, I was interested in architecture. My best subject at school, the one I enjoyed most, was Graphic communication. I decided to try to get a career using that. So, I went into an architect's office and was there for four years before I decided to start my HND.

The course – part 2

I Tell me about your timetable.
A I have classes three days a week – Monday, Wednesday, and Friday, and Self-study on the other days.
I Which subject appeals to you most?
A Erm, the Theory of structures. I really enjoy it. That's twice on a Monday – Monday morning first thing and on Monday afternoon.
I What do you like about it?
A I like the maths and physics side of it, how the structure actually works.
I Is any of the work in the lab?
A We've got Materials this semester. We're in the lab every week – testing concrete and that sort of thing. On Fridays, there's Project work from 11.15 for most of the day. I've been at a structural engineering company learning how a civil engineering project is run.
I What's the company working on?
A They're turning an old office building into a nightclub, restaurant, and five-star hotel. It's interesting to get on site and to speak to the engineers.
I What's Complex communications on Wednesday?
A Before and after lunch? It's about language. You have to pick something to do with engineering and write a report about it. Then present it to the other students.
I What have you chosen?
A I'm doing a project on a new bridge over the Forth, right here in Scotland. There's

a lot of public opposition.
I Do we need a new bridge?
A Yes, the research I've done shows the present bridge is carrying ten times the amount of traffic it was designed for.
I What's Fluid mechanics on Friday morning?
A Er, it's how fluids behave, water pressure on pipes, and that sort of thing. It's one of the hardest subjects.
I Do you find you have a lot of work to do outside the course?
A Yes, it's not particularly hard but it's constant.
I And how is it assessed?
A It's modular, continuous assessment. You have to pass all the modules.

The course – part 3

I What do you hope to do at the end of your course?
A Well, I want to go on to do the degree.
I What kind of degree will you take?
A I'd like to do Structural engineering, a BEng. I've got acceptance from two universities. I can start once I've finished one year of my HND.
I How long will it take?
A It's four years for a BEng.
I When you start work as a Civil Engineer, what do you want to build – houses or big structures like bridges and roads?
A I'm more interested in the big structures like bridges.
I You may have to go overseas for that.
A That's one reason why I chose this career. That you can travel. There's a lot of opportunities to go overseas.

Pronunciation – Strong and weak forms of auxiliary verbs

1

Does Alec like Maths?   Yes, he *does*.
Is he in his first year?   Yes, he *is*.

3

1 Is he studying to be an engineer?
   Yes, he *is*.
2 Are there any women in his class?
   No, there *aren't*.
3 Does his course take two years?
   Yes, it *does*.
4 Can he start a degree after six months?
   No, he *can't*.

5 Has he got acceptance from two universities?   Yes, he *has*.

6 Does he have to pass all the modules? Yes, he *does*.

7 Will it take him four years to complete the BEng?   Yes, it *will*.

8 Has he got any lab work on his course? Yes, he *has*.

Unit 3

Listening – The design process

I start with a design brief – a description of the problem I'm going to solve. In this case, it's to design a backpack for cross-country skiers. Then I investigate, and do some research about cross-country skiers, the things they need to carry and the weight they find comfortable. I also think about the best choice of material – waterproof, hard-wearing, easy to work with. Next, I sketch different shapes for the backpack and choose what I think is the best solution. I transfer my sketch to a computer to make a proper drawing with all the dimensions in place. Then, I ask a company to realize it and make up some prototypes to test how well it works. Finally, I compare the product with the brief. I evaluate it by asking questions like: *Does it meet all the requirements? Can I make it any better, or improve it somehow?*

Listening – Working with design

A Karl

I design practical products for use in the home, especially the kitchen. When I'm designing, I think about the function of the object and how people will use it. Then I sketch my ideas on paper, starting with the shape. I make lots of these rough drawings until I get the shape that I want.

B Martin

I'm an Industrial Designer. I design mass-produced products. I always have to balance what people need and what it's possible to make. I start with a sketch and when I'm happy with the result, I plan the basic layout on a computer. Then I print out technical drawings to make templates. I use the templates to cut out a model in foam plastic. This gives me an idea of the shape and look of the object.

C Hilary

I'm a product developer. I have to work with the designers on the one hand and the manufacturers on the other. And I have to keep both of them happy to get good designs which can be produced at prices people can afford. I get the drawings and models from the designers, talk to the manufacturers about the production, and work out the costings.

Unit 4

Pronunciation – Intonation for questions

1
Where are you from?
What do you study?

2
Are you Italian?
Do you speak English?

3
A What materials do we use for ski poles?
B Aluminium or carbon-fibre, I think. What are footballs made of?
A I'm not sure. Is it leather?
B Yes, I'm certain. What's used to make bobsleighs?

Listening – Exchanging information

A OK, so tell me about the skateboard.
B Right. The body part is the deck.
A What's it made of?
B Plywood. This means it's light and strong.
A OK. What's the difference between the front and back?
B The front is called the nose. And the back is the tail.
A Nose and tail. Right.
B There's an angle of twenty degrees.
A What for?
B It helps the skateboarder perform tricks.
A Cool. So, what about under the board?
B These things are the trucks.
A What are they made of? Metal?
B Yes – sometimes it's titanium for strength. The top is called the baseplate.
The bottom is the hanger.
A Got it. And the wheels – they're plastic, right?
B Right. They're made of polyurethane. The hardness varies. Very hard wheels are good for performance. Is that it?
A What about these? Are they springs, like a car suspension?
B Oh yes, they're called bushings. They help you to turn the board …

B … I think I know a bit about the snowboard. Is it made of fibreglass?
A Yeah, partly. But wood is used for the core.
B Really? How come?
A It gives the board strength but keeps it light. And it makes it flexible.
B OK. Is it the same on both sides?
A The base, the bottom, is covered with a kind of tough plastic.
B What's it called?
A *P-tex*. It helps the board slide but it's wear-resistant.
B Right. Important on snow. What about the edge? Is it made of *p-tex* as well?
A No, that's steel. It helps the board grip the snow.
B When it turns and does tricks?
A Yeah, I suppose so.
B OK. Oh, and these straps – are they made of nylon?
A Yeah. They're called bindings. That's it.

Unit 5

Switch on

This is a wind pump. It's used for pumping water from under the ground. As you can see, it's a very simple mechanism. The wind turns the blades. This rotary movement is converted into an up-and-down movement by the crankshaft – just like the crankshaft in a car engine. The piston of the pump is connected to the crankshaft. As the blades rotate, water is pumped from the well.

It's used in the developing world, for example in Africa and in parts of India. This particular wind pump is in Kenya. It can be used to provide drinking water or water for crops.

This is an example of appropriate technology. It's low cost. It doesn't use expensive fuel. It's made from inexpensive materials and it can be repaired easily. It's the right technology for the situation.

Pairwork

This is a solar water distiller. It's actually quite easy to make. It's for producing clean, drinkable water from dirty water. It uses the heat of the sun. The still is filled with dirty water via the inlet at the base. The black bottom absorbs heat from the sun and warms the water. The reflector increases the amount of heat reaching the water. The heat helps to kill anything harmful in the water. The hot water evaporates and condenses on the inside of the glass cover. This condensed water is clean and safe to drink. The cover is tilted to the south so the condensed water runs down and collects in the fresh water trough. With a glass cover of about a square metre, the still can produce almost four litres of clean water every five hours. You have to clean out the still regularly to remove any sediment, but you can also use the cleaning water to irrigate plants.

Pronunciation – Numbers and quantities

1
a three point one four two
b eleven hundred and fifty millimetres
c two hundred and fifty megabytes
d sixty gigabytes
e sixteen kilohertz
f thirty milliamps
g zero degrees Celsius
h seventy-three per cent
i twelve volts DC
j ten to the power six
k ten to the power minus twelve
l a ratio of forty to one

2
a minus two hundred and seventy-three point one five degrees Celsius
b ninety-five point eight megahertz
c one hundred and ten volts AC
d two to the power twenty
e one million, forty-eight thousand, five hundred and seventy-six
f a ratio of one to eight
g sixteen millimetres
h zero point zero one
i thirteen point five per cent
j two hundred and fifty-six gigabytes

Unit 6

Listening – Crime-fighting equipment

As a police officer, technology helps me work safely and more efficiently. Every police officer who's out on duty carries, or wears, plenty of equipment – both low-tech and high-tech. For example, we all carry a torch. It's lightweight and metal, so not easily broken. It's very useful. A lot of incidents happen in dark places, and you can use it to signal to traffic if there's a traffic accident at night.

We all have handcuffs – still the simplest way to restrain someone. You can cuff their hands together, or cuff them to something solid like a gate or even to another person. The type we have are called 'quickcuffs' because you can use them very easily.

In the UK, not all police officers are licensed to carry firearms – guns and so on – but all of us have batons. They're made from polycarbonate so they're strong but not heavy to carry. They extend to keep people at a safe distance. We also have CS gas canisters. If someone gets violent, CS will incapacitate them for a short time. And we wear knife-proof vests, a kind of body armour made of Kevlar.

Some police forces are experimenting with stun guns, tasers, for use against suspects armed with a dangerous weapon, like a knife. They give a powerful electric shock.

We all carry radios so we can contact each other and police headquarters at any time. We can get help quickly or information about a suspect. And of course, we all have a notebook. The function of that is obvious!

Unit 7

It's my job

I work in a large plant bakery. We make bread for supermarkets. Most of the bread people eat in the UK comes from plants like this. My job is to keep the plant running, to maintain all the machinery. If anything goes wrong, it's my

responsibility to get the plant going again.

The entire process is computer-controlled. These are the main stages. First, 225 kilogrammes of flour, water, yeast, fat, and other ingredients are mixed in a steel mixer for three minutes to make dough. Then the dough is cut into loaves, put into tins and left for 54 minutes in a prover for the yeast to work. After that, the loaves are baked in giant gas ovens for precisely 21 minutes. Next, they're left to cool for 110 minutes, and then taken out of their tins using suction. Then they're sprayed with a chemical to keep them fresh longer. Next, the loaves are sliced in a high-speed slicer with giant saw blades. Finally, they're wrapped by the wrapping machine and sent to the supermarkets.

The process never stops. Our bakery produces 10,000 loaves per hour – that's 240,000 per day!

Unit 8

It's my job

I work for a Polish company which converts diesel engines to run on natural gas. They're used in forklifts and tractors, but mostly in buses. Diesel-engine buses can produce a lot of pollution. The air quality in city centres is often quite poor. Natural gas–fuelled engines are much cleaner than diesel. The work that we do is helping to improve the air quality in our cities.

In the past few years, we've started to build gas-powered generators. They produce up to 100 kilowatts. They run on biogas from sewage treatment plants. They produce all the power the plant needs, and more. When there's a power cut, people find it a bit strange that the sewage plant has all its lights on.

I travel quite a lot in my job. I help to install new generators all over the country and to provide support for bus companies who use our engines. We're planning to export to other EU countries so I might have more opportunity to travel outside Poland and maybe use my English.

Pronunciation – Corrective stress

1

A Electric motors aren't very efficient.

B No, electric motors *are* very efficient.

2

1

A Hybrid cars have a diesel engine and an electric motor.

B No, hybrid cars have a *petrol* engine and an electric motor.

2

A Hydrogen fuel cells are cheap.

B No, hydrogen fuel cells *aren't* cheap.

3

A Most car drivers are happy to use public transport.

B No, most car drivers *aren't* happy to use public transport.

4

A LPG cuts down pollution a lot.

B No, LPG cuts down pollution a *little*.

5

A ASVs are more dangerous for pedestrians.

B No, ASVs are *safer* for pedestrians.

6

A Solar power is the answer to our transport problems.

B No, solar power *isn't* the answer to our transport problems.

7

A Air travel is good for the environment.

B No, air travel *isn't* good for the environment.

8

A Trains and cars are examples of public transport.

B No, trains and *buses* are examples of public transport.

Unit 9

It's my job

I'm self-employed but I work with three other guys as a gang – that's like a team. We get contracts from construction companies, maybe a few weeks, maybe a year. It depends on the size of the building. You have to be prepared to travel wherever the work is but the money is good. There are bonuses too, for finishing ahead of schedule.

What we do is we build the steel frames of all sorts of buildings. I've worked on supermarkets, warehouses, and multi-storey buildings, including one that was 30 storeys high.

Everything is pre-fabricated. The steel is cut to the right size and drilled before it comes to the site. We have to bolt or weld the pieces together. It sounds easy but try lining up a one-tonne girder swinging from a crane on a winter's day when you're a hundred metres up! We like to work fast, and to do that you need ground people who make sure everything reaches you in the right order, and a crane operator who can deliver on the spot – right where you need it.

On a typical day, I could be working a twelve-hour shift. If you're high up, you don't come down for tea-breaks. Everything you need is up there – canteen, toilets.

Is it dangerous? Well, yes, but there *are* a lot of safety precautions. We have to wear a safety harness with a lifeline. There are safety cables slung round whichever floor you're working on, and you clip on to one as soon as you start. There's a safety net underneath the floor until the deck is down. For me, the most dangerous time is moving the girders into the right position. You could be crushed.

I'd like to set up my own construction company eventually, and employ others to do this kind of work.

Pronunciation – Stress in long words (1)

1

a aluminium

b component

c construction

d defective

e installed

f powered

g precaution

h prefabricated

i reinforced

j skyscraper

k temperatures

l visibility

3

1 appropriate emergencies
  developing kilometre

2 automatic horizontal regulation
  exploration polystyrene unfamiliar

3 designated helicopter supermarket
  generator operator

Unit 10

It's my job

My special area is electronic assistive technology, or EAT for short. I work for a company which makes equipment to help severely disabled people. I mean people who can't walk, people who have very limited movement – perhaps they can move only their head.

We make equipment which helps these people to live as independently as possible. By moving their chin, by blowing down a tube, or simply by speaking, they can send an email, adjust the temperature in the room, or operate a TV.

In this kind of work, you need a knowledge of mechatronics. That's where mechanics, electronics, and software engineering meet. Take a page-turner, for example. It's a device which turns the pages of a book or magazine. The input can be a pneumatic switch – that's a switch worked by air pressure. You operate it by sucking or blowing down a tube. These signals are interpreted by a microprocessor which controls the mechanism which turns the pages. That mechanism uses electrical and mechanical devices. All three branches of engineering combine to make it work.

It's an exciting job. Each development in technology means new possibilities for disabled people.

Pronunciation – Linking words

1 a door opener

3

1 a curtain opener

2 a window opener

3 a personal alarm

4 a remote control

5 a light switch

6 a domestic appliance

7 a gear box

8 a diesel engine

9 a digital radio

10 an MP3 player

Unit 11

Listening – Opinions

I=Interviewer, M=Max, S=Sam

I Max, how do you listen to music?

M Live, of course, but I also listen to music online. I go to Napster and search for music I like.

I Can you listen first and decide if you want to pay for a track?

M Yes, if you don't like it you can skip it. If you do like it, you can download it to your hard drive or burn it to a CD.

I Sam, how do you listen to music?

S CDs, albums, MP3 player, minidisks sometimes, and online. You can have music now anytime and anywhere you want it.

I What's so special about this way of listening?

S You can make your own music library on your hard drive or MP3 player. You can have a playlist of tracks you listen to when you get up, or a playlist for when you travel to work, or when you want to relax in the evening. Some MP3 players will decide what you like listening to and arrange the tracks for you. You can exchange tracks with friends – it's illegal but everybody does it.

I I read that more than seven million people here in Britain regularly download their music from illegal sites.

M That's just theft on a huge scale. It's damaging music – music for the future. It cheats the musicians and the recording companies. People who download illegally are buying fewer albums and far fewer singles. It's hurting the music industry.

I Is it just teenagers who're doing this?

M No, it's all sorts of people.

I What should the music industry do?

M Set up their own sites for selling music online. Go after anyone who downloads illegally.

I What do you think, Sam?

S CDs are over-priced. I don't see why we shouldn't share tracks with friends.

Unit 12

Listening – Describing changes

L=Laura, J=Journalist

L Well, we're much more efficient now. In the past, cans were made from three pieces of metal: sides, top, and bottom. Now, it's just two. The sides and bottom are made from one piece. It's a much faster process and less metal is used. We used to get 50 cans from every kilo of aluminium, now we get 75 – and half the aluminium is from recycled cans.

J OK. What about other changes? Is there anything the average customer would notice?

L Well, we've introduced pull tabs on all our range, so can openers are almost a thing of the past. In the past, paper labels were applied at the canning plants. Now we can print directly onto the can whatever our customers want.

J What about your workforce? Any changes there?

L Our workforce is smaller. About half the number who were employed ten years ago.

Customer care – Working on a help desk

J=John, A=Alex

J Hello. Help desk, John speaking. How can I help?

A Hi, it's Alex from Accounts. We've got a problem with our printer.

J What make is it?

A It's a Hewlett Packard.

J OK, it's an HP. What model is it?

A It's a LaserJet 2400.

J Thanks. What exactly is the problem?

A I had a paper jam. I've cleared it but it won't print and the orange light is on.

J Mm-hm. Is there paper in the printer?

A Yes, I've refilled it.

J All right. In the bottom left of your screen you'll see the 'Start' button. Click on it. Choose 'Settings', then 'Printers'. OK?

A Yes.

J You should see your printer listed. Double click on it. What does it say under 'Status'?

A Er, 'Printing paused'.

J Ah, click on 'Printer' and choose 'Purge

print document'. That should clear it. It may take a few seconds. Then try to print again.

A … OK, ah, that's cleared it. Thanks a lot. Bye.

J No problem. Bye.

Pronunciation – -ed form of verbs and words with silent letters

1

1	constructed	9	mixed
2	controlled	10	operated
3	customized	11	planned
4	damaged	12	produced
5	disabled	13	reflected
6	finished	14	searched
7	integrated	15	worked
8	invented		

2

/t/

finished   mixed   produced   searched   worked

/d/

controlled   customized   damaged   disabled   planned

/ɪd/

constructed   integrated   invented   operated   reflected

5

1	listening	4	pneumatic	7	would
2	might	5	should		
3	modelling	6	vehicle		

Unit 13

It's my job

I'm a Telecommunications Technician. I work for a company which provides phone systems for business use, especially banks. I've been with the company for eight years. Before that, I was in the army for four years. I joined when I left school. I was in Signals. They trained me to set up and maintain mobile communications equipment – satellite dishes, antennas, VHF radios, that sort of thing. I enjoyed my time in the army – mostly because I travelled quite a lot. I've been to Norway, Kenya, and Belize.

I've seen quite a few changes in phone systems. We've replaced copper cables with fibre-optic networks. The most important one now is the change to VoIP. That's Voice over Internet Protocol. Basically, it's a system that allows voice signals to be sent via the Internet. You can make long distance calls cheaply.

In general, telecommunications equipment has become more complex, more powerful in the data it can handle – and lighter. My job used to be 70% brain and 30% muscle. Now, it's 90% brain and 10% muscle!

Most of my work is indoors though. It's not just installing and testing equipment – I have to explain to clients how to use the new systems. Being able to explain quite complicated technology in simple terms is an important part of my work. That's one of the things I enjoy most.

Sometimes I have to work outdoors to bring a line into a building or fix a dish on the roof. It's great in summer but it's not much fun if it's pouring with rain!

Pronunciation – Past Simple v Present Perfect

1 They've spent time in the army.
2 I've texted him an invitation.
3 He's faxed me a reply.
4 Todd phoned the office.
5 She emailed me twice.

Customer care – Explaining in simple terms

The CD and the DVD are both types of media for storing information. Erm, they look exactly the same. They're the same size and shape but they have different storage space. The DVD can store a lot more than the CD. Erm, so you would tend to use CDs for storing text and sound whereas if you want video, which takes a lot more space, you would tend to use DVD. The way that the information is stored on CDs and DVDs, written to them and read from them, is different so you need different drives for reading and writing to them. Both of them are optical devices. They use laser light. A DVD drive can read and write to CDs but a CD drive can't read or write to a DVD.

Unit 14

Pronunciation – Stress in long words (2)

1
a computer
b co-operative
c download
d hydraulic
e microprocessor
f petroleum
g prototype
h simulator
i supercomputer
j telecommunications
k ultrasound
l vibrate

2
animator
anticlockwise
capacity
dependable
development
energetic
enterprising
entertainment
environment
indicator
information
motivated
peripheral
simulation
ventilated

Speaking – Job interview

I=Interviewer, A=Applicant
I What experience do you have in this kind of work?
A I'm a skilled carpenter and I've done a lot of work making displays for exhibitions and conferences. It's quite similar to stage work.
I Do you have any experience working with lighting or sound systems?
A I was a roadie with a rock band for six months. The band didn't last very long – they weren't very good – but I got a lot of experience with sound systems.
I We're looking for someone who's prepared to travel for at least four months each year. Would that be a problem for you?
A No, I'm single at the moment, and I like travelling.
I Why do you think you're the right person for the job?
A I've got relevant experience. I like variety in my work. I'm good at problem-solving.
I Are there any questions you would like to ask us?
A Yes, how many technicians do you employ? And, of course …

Unit 15

Listening – Predictions

I=Interviewer, L=Lianne, S=Stefan
I This week on *The monitor*, we have Lianne Bradley and Stefan Werner with us. They're both futurologists. They advise companies on the most likely future trends. Our topic is the future of technology. Lianne, what's your view about the way things will go?
L On the plus side, good things will happen in health. Computers will find out what's wrong with us by asking questions and carrying out tests. Robots will operate on us with better precision than humans. However, as always with technology, we'll find new military uses. We'll get better at killing each other from a distance with unmanned aircraft and smart weapons programmed to recognize their targets. In telecommunications, we'll make our phone calls through the Internet. Everybody will be able to be a reporter. If you see anything important, you'll be able to transmit it to the rest of the world. In computing, the keyboard will disappear. Everything will be voice-operated. In our homes, we might also have voice-operated domestic appliances. We'll tell the oven how we like our pizza and it will remember the next time we ask it to bake one. I'm not optimistic about the developing world. Poorer countries will fall further behind unless they can invest heavily in education.
I Mm-hm. Stefan, where do you think there'll be big changes?
S The greatest changes will take place in IT. I'll name just a few. Computers will be faster and more powerful, and they'll be everywhere including in the clothes we wear. Wearable computers will give us directions, act as phones, and search the Internet for information we want. They'll find real answers, not just a list of web pages to try. On the downside, I expect digital crime will increase. For example, stealing someone's identity to get into their internet bank account or creating a virus to close down a business. In

transport, I think we'll see the development of cheaper fuel cells so that cars and motorbikes can run on hydrogen. I don't agree with Lianne about the developing world though. Developing countries will go straight to the new technologies without working through the old. We've seen this already with mobile phones in Africa. Instead of developing lots of expensive land lines first, African countries have gone straight to mobile phones. New technologies will help to produce better crops and will require little expensive energy.

I Thanks, and speaking of energy, how do you both suppose energy requirements will be met in the future?

Pronunciation – Linking in phrasal verbs

1
Set it up.
Cut them off.

2

1	Line them up.	6	Shut it down.
2	Give it up.	7	Start it up.
3	Work it out.	8	Print them out.
4	Switch it off.	9	Plug it in.
5	Find it out.	10	Turn it on.

Glossary

Vowels

iː	screen	ʊ	function	aɪ	hybrid
i	accuracy	uː	cool	aʊ	download
ɪ	chip	u	evaluate	ɔɪ	coil
e	network	ʌ	buckle	ɪə	experience
æ	alloy	ɜː	convert	eə	bearings
ɑː	hardware	ə	grinder	ʊə	security
ɒ	bonding	eɪ	delay		
ɔː	former	əʊ	bonus		

Consonants

p	pulley	f	fuel	h	hopper
b	barrel	v	virus	m	model
t	tagging	θ	thrust	n	antenna
d	dish	ð	leather	ŋ	bonding
k	code	s	support	l	laminate
g	grip	z	supervise	r	ram
tʃ	charge	ʃ	dish	j	yeast
dʒ	joystick	ʒ	corrosion	w	wear

accelerator /əkˈseləreɪtə(r)/ *n* the foot pedal of a car that controls the speed

accuracy /ˈækjərəsi/ *n* precision, exactness, or correctness

adaptor /əˈdæptə(r)/ *n* a device which allows electrical equipment to be used in conditions other than those it was designed for

aerodynamic /ˌeərədaɪˈnæmɪk/ *adj* designed to reduce wind resistance

affect /əˈfekt/ *v* to influence something or cause a change in something

alloy /ˈælɔɪ/ *n* a metal that consists of two or more different metals mixed together

animator /ˈænɪmeɪtə(r)/ *n* an artist who makes drawings or models appear to move as if they were alive

antenna /ænˈtenə/ *n* an aerial for sending or receiving signals

architecture /ˈɑːkɪtektʃə(r)/ *n* the science of designing buildings

artificial /ˌɑːtɪˈfɪʃl/ *adj* made as a copy of something natural; man-made

assembly line /əˈsembli laɪn/ *n* an arrangement of machines and workers to create a product

automatic /ˌɔːtəˈmætɪk/ *adj* able to work by itself

automatically /ˌɔːtəˈmætɪkli/ *adv* working by itself without human intervention

barrel /ˈbærəl/ *n* a hollow, usually cylindrical, machine part

bearings /ˈbeərɪŋgz/ *n* machine parts that are designed to reduce friction between moving parts

blade /bleɪd/ *n* the cutting part of a machine or tool

blurred vision /ˌblɜːd ˈvɪʒn/ *n* inability to see things clearly

body armour /ˈbɒdi ˈɑːmə(r)/ *n* protective covering

bonding /ˈbɒndɪŋ/ *n* sticking things together using adhesive

bonus /ˈbəʊnəs/ *n* an additional amount of money added to wages as a reward

brief /briːf/ *n* instructions and information given to somebody before they do a piece of work

broadband /ˈbrɔːdbænd/ *n* a system that allows large amounts of electronic data to be sent at high speed

buckle /ˈbʌkl/ *v* to be forced out of shape by heat

CADCAM /ˈkædkæm/ *n* Computer-aided design and Computer-aided manufacturing

calculate /ˈkælkjəleɪt/ *v* to use numbers to find out a total number, amount, distance, etc.

career /kəˈrɪə(r)/ *n* a job or profession for which you are trained

carpentry /ˈkɑːpəntri/ *n* making things from wood; the work of a carpenter

charge (batteries) /ˌtʃɑːdʒ ˈbætrɪz/ *v* to cause batteries to take in and store electricity

chip /tʃɪp/ *n* a small electronic component containing an integrated circuit; a microchip

CIM /ˌsiː aɪ ˈem/ *n* Computer-integrated manufacturing

cladding /ˈklædɪŋ/ *n* the material used for the external lining of the building

clip /klɪp/ *n* a short piece of a longer recording of sound or film

CNC /ˌsiː en ˈsiː/ *n* Computer numerical control

code /kəʊd/ *n* a set of programme instructions

coil /kɔɪl/ *n* wire formed into a continuous series of circles to carry an electrical current

colour-blind /ˈkʌlə blaɪnd/ *adj* unable to see the difference between certain colours

compatible /kəmˈpætɪbl/ *adj* able to work together

competences /ˈkɒmpətənsɪz/ *n* the abilities or skills needed for a particular task or job

complex /ˈkɒmpleks/ *adj* complicated; not simple

composites /ˈkɒmpəsɪts/ *n* fibre-reinforced plastics; materials made up of different materials

compress /kəmˈpres/ *v* to make computer data take up as little space as possible

compression /kəmˈpreʃn/ *n* the process of forcing a substance into less space, and therefore increasing its internal pressure

computer file /kəmˈpjuːtə faɪl/ *n* a collection of information stored under a particular name in a computer

congestion /kənˈdʒestʃn/ *n* the state of being too full of traffic

construction /kənˈstrʌkʃn/ *n* building; the work of the building industry

convert /kənˈvɜːt/ *v* to change something from one form or system to another

cool /kuːl/ *v* to transfer heat from something

corrosion /kəˈrəʊʒn/ *n* destruction or damage caused by chemical action

costings /ˈkɒstɪŋz/ *n* a calculation of the cost of design and manufacture of a product

course /kɔːs/ *n* a programme of study in a particular subject

crankshaft /ˈkræŋkʃɑːft/ *n* the main shaft of an engine, which is driven by the cranks or cam rods and transforms rotating movement into up and down movement, or up and down movement to rotating movement

customized /ˈkʌstəmaɪzd/ *adj* built or changed according to what a particular customer wants

CV /ˌsiː ˈviː/ *n* (curriculum vitae) a written record of your education and the jobs you have done that you send when you are applying for a job

decking /ˈdekɪŋ/ *n* sheets of material used to make a platform

defect /ˈdiːfekt/ *n* a fault or imperfection

delay /dɪˈleɪ/ *n* a problem that makes something slow or late

detect /dɪˈtekt/ *v* to notice or discover something

dish /dɪʃ/ *n* a directional antenna with a concave surface

domestic appliance /dəˌmestɪk əˈplaɪəns/ *n* a machine or gadget for use in the home

download /ˈdaʊnləʊd/ *v* to transfer data to your computer from the Internet

efficient /ɪˈfɪʃnt/ *adj* working well or quickly, without waste

engage (gears) /ɪnˈgeɪdʒ/ *v* when gears engage, they fit together and start to work

escape /ɪsˈkeɪp/ *v* to get away from something

evaluate /ɪˈvæljueɪt/ *v* to judge the value of something

exhaust gas /ɪgˈzɔːst gæs/ *n* waste gas discharged from an engine

experience /ɪksˈpɪəriəns/ *n* knowledge gained by doing something

exploration /ˌekspləˈreɪʃn/ *n* travel that is done in order to find out about new places, to find resources such as oil, etc.

extrusion /eksˈtruːʒn/ *n* the operation of producing solid and hollow sections by forcing material through a die

flammable /ˈflæməbl/ *adj* that can be set on fire

flexible /ˈfleksɪbl/ *adj* that can bend or be bent easily

former /ˈfɔːmə(r)/ *n* something that is used to provide shape, that can be removed after use

fuel /fjuːl/ *n* petrol or other material that is used to produce power by burning

fuel cell /ˈfjuːl sel/ *n* a battery which produces electricity by combining a fuel with oxygen

function /ˈfʌŋkʃn/ *n* the purpose or use that something has

games console /ˈgeɪmz ˌkɒnsəʊl/ *n* an electronic device designed for playing video games

generate /ˈdʒenəreɪt/ *v* to produce electricity

girder /ˈgɜːdə(r)/ *n* a beam, usually steel, that bridges an open space

give up /gɪv ˈʌp/ *v* to stop having or doing something

global warming /ˌgləʊbl ˈwɔːmɪŋ/ *n* a rise in the temperature of the earth's atmosphere

GPS /ˌdʒiː piː ˈes/ *n* Global positioning system; a system that uses satellite signals to show you your exact position

grinder /ˈgraɪndə(r)/ *n* a machine that uses an abrasive to remove material from a hard surface

grip /grɪp/ *n* ability to hold onto a surface; the way in which you hold something in your hand

guard /gɑːd/ *n* a safety device that covers part of a machine in order to prevent injury

hack /hæk/ *v* if you hack into a computer system, you access it without permission, for example in order to steal something

hard disk /ˌhɑːd ˈdɪsk/ *n* a mass storage device for digital data

hardware /ˈhɑːdweə(r)/ *n* the electronic and electrical parts of a computer

hopper /ˈhɒpə(r)/ *n* a funnel through which plastic beads pass to the barrel in an injection-moulding machine

hybrid /ˈhaɪbrɪd/ *adj* (used about cars) using two different forms of power

hydraulic /haɪˈdrɒlɪk/ *adj* operated by the pressure of water or another fluid

image /ˈɪmɪdʒ/ *n* a picture

in orbit /ɪn ˈɔːbɪt/ *adv* moving round the earth in space

incapacitate /ˌɪnkəˈpæsɪteɪt/ *v* to make somebody unable to do anything

ingredients /ɪnˈgriːdiənts/ *n* the things that are put together to make something

innovation /ˌɪnəˈveɪʃn/ *n* a new idea, method, or invention; the introduction of new things

inspect /ɪnˈspekt/ *v* to examine something for faults

interact /ˌɪntərˈækt/ *v* to have an effect on something or somebody else by being or working together

interview /ˈɪntəvjuː/ *n* a formal meeting at which somebody is asked questions to see if they are suitable for a particular job

intranet /ˈɪntrənet/ *n* a computer network that is private to a company or organization

investigate /ɪnˈvestɪgeɪt/ *v* to study and try different things in order to find the solution you want

joystick /ˈdʒɔɪstɪk/ *n* an upright handle that is moved to control the operation of something

lab /læb/ *n* a laboratory; a special building or room for studying science subjects

laminate /ˈlæmɪneɪt/ *n* a strong material made by joining many thin sheets of material on top of each other

lifeline /ˈlaɪflaɪn/ *n* a safety device used to attach a worker to a secure point

lighting /ˈlaɪtɪŋ/ *n* the system, arrangement, or equipment that lights a room, or the quality of the light produced

liquefied /ˈlɪkwɪfaɪd/ *adj* changed into a liquid

low-tech /ˌləʊ ˈtek/ *adj* using simple technology

machine tool /məˈʃiːn tuːl/ *n* a power-driven tool for cutting or shaping metals, wood, etc.

machining /məˈʃiːnɪŋ/ *n* cutting or shaping metals or wood by machinery

maintenance /ˈmeɪntənəns/ *n* regular checks and repairs done to keep something in good condition

manufacturer /ˌmanjʊˈfæktʃərə(r)/ *n* a firm that makes goods

manufacturing /ˌmanjʊˈfæktʃərɪŋ/ *n* making or producing goods by machinery or other industrial process, usually in large quantities

mass-produce /ˌmæs prəˈdjuːs/ *v* to manufacture something in large quantities

missile /ˈmɪsaɪl/ *n* an explosive flying weapon, with its own engine, that can be aimed at a distant object

model /ˌmɒdl/ *n* a three-dimensional image or prototype used as part of the design process

monitor /ˈmɒnɪtə(r)/ *v* to watch and check something over a period of time

motion sensor /ˈməʊʃn ˌsensə(r)/ *n* a device which detects movement

mould /məʊld/ *n* a shaped container into which you put soft material or liquid, which becomes solid in the shape of the container when it is cooled

network /ˈnetwɜːk/ *n* a number of computers and other devices that are connected together so that equipment and information can be shared

off-shore /ˌɒf ˈʃɔː(r)/ *adj* in the sea, at a distance from the shore

off-site /ˌɒf ˈsaɪt/ *adv* away from the workplace

online /ɒnˈlaɪn/ *adj* using the Internet or existing on the Internet

overseas /ˌəʊvəˈsiːz/ *adv* to another country; abroad

performance /pəˈfɔːməns/ *n* how well something works; an occasion when people come to listen to somebody making music

peripheral /pəˈrɪfərəl/ *n* an input or output device linked to a computer

pile /paɪl/ *n* a pillar which is sunk into the ground to support vertical loading

PIN /pɪn/ *n* Personal identification number; a number given to you, for example by a bank, so that you can take money from a cash machine or pay for goods using a card

plant /plɑːnt/ *n* heavy machinery, especially used in an industrial process

plating /ˈpleɪtɪŋ/ *n* covering a material with a thin layer of metal

plywood /ˈplaɪwʊd/ *n* a material consisting of a number of thin layers of wood glued together so that the natural direction of the wood in each layer is at 90° to the direction in the next layer

pneumatic /njuːˈmætɪk/ *adj* operated by air pressure

pollution /pəˈluːʃn/ *n* substances or actions that change the environment in a bad way

portable /ˈpɔːtəbl/ *adj* that can be easily carried or moved

power station /ˈpaʊə ˌsteɪʃn/ *n* a large building in which electricity is generated

prediction /prɪˈdɪkʃn/ *n* a statement that says what you think will happen

prefabricated /ˌpriːˈfæbrɪkeɪtɪd/ *adj* already made, in order to be put together later in another place

present /prɪˈzent/ *v* to talk about a subject to an audience

process /ˈprəʊses/ *n* a series of actions performed in order to make something

processor /ˈprəʊsesə(r)/ *n* the part of a computer that controls all the other parts of the system

product /ˈprɒdʌkt/ n a thing that is manufactured

production /prəˈdʌkʃn/ n the process of making goods or materials

program /ˈprəʊɡræm/ n a set of instructions in code that controls the operations and functions of a computer

project management /ˈprɒdʒekt ˌmænɪdʒmənt/ n the process of planning, organizing, and controlling tasks, costs, staff, and resources so that a project is completed in a successful way

property /ˈprɒpəti:/ n a quality or attribute of a material

prototype /ˈprəʊtətaɪp/ n the first form of something

public transport /ˌpʌblɪk ˈtrɑːnspɔːt/ n transport such as buses or trains that are provided for everybody

pulley /ˈpʌli/ n a grooved wheel for transmitting power by means of a belt

pump /pʌmp/ n, v a machine for forcing liquids or a gas into or out of something

pvc /ˌpiː viː ˈsiː/ n Polyvinyl chloride; the best known and most widely used vinyl plastic

qualification /ˌkwɒlɪfɪˈkeɪʃn/ n an examination that you have passed or a course that you have completed

ram /ræm/ n part of a machine that pushes onto or into something

ratio /ˈreɪʃiəʊ/ n the relationship between two things, represented by two numbers showing how much larger one thing is than the other

realistic /ˌriːəˈlɪstɪk/ adj like in real life

rechargeable /riːˈtʃɑːdʒəbl/ adj capable of taking a new charge of electricity

recognition /ˌrekəɡˈnɪʃn/ n the ability to identify somebody or something from individual characteristics

recording studio /rɪˈkɔːdɪŋ ˌstjuːdiəʊ/ n a room where sound recordings are made

reflect /rɪˈflekt/ v to throw back an image, light, sound, or heat

replace /rɪˈpleɪs/ v to substitute something with a new or different thing

report /rɪˈpɔːt/ v to give an account of an event

requirement /rɪˈkwaɪəmnt/ n something that is needed

research /ˈriːsɜːtʃ/ n investigation aimed at finding out new information

rival /ˈraɪvl/ n a company, product, etc. that is in competition with another

rocket /ˈrɒkɪt/ n a missile projected through the air by a jet of gas

router /ˈruːtə(r)/ n a device that directs data from one computer system to another in the shortest possible time

rural /ˈrʊərəl/ adj in the countryside, away from big towns or cities

safety harness /ˈseɪfti ˌhɑːnəs/ n a safety device worn to prevent you from falling from a height

satellite /ˈsætəlaɪt/ n a device that travels around the earth, receiving signals and transmitting them back to earth

satellite receiver /ˈsætəlaɪt rɪˌsiːvə(r)/ n a TV or radio capable of receiving signals broadcast via satellite

saw /sɔː/ n any machine or tool with a thin, toothed blade for cutting hard materials

scanner /ˈskænə(r)/ n a device that copies images in a form that can be processed on a computer

screen /skriːn/ n the viewing surface of a television or computer monitor

security /sɪˈkjʊərəti/ n the activities involved in protecting something or somebody

sell-by date /ˈsel baɪ ˌdeɪt/ n the date after which a product must not be offered for sale

semester /sɪˈmestə(r)/ n one of the two periods that the school or college year is divided into

semiconductor /ˌsemikənˈdʌktə(r)/ n an electronic device such as a transistor which forms the basis of all integrated circuits

sensor /ˈsensə(r)/ n a device used to detect the presence of a particular quality or effect such as heat, light, sound, etc.

setting /ˈsetɪŋ/ n the position at which a control is set

shock /ʃɒk/ n sudden violent movement or contact with something

simulated /ˈsɪmjəleɪtɪd/ adj done on a computer, in a way that creates real-life conditions

simulation /ˌsɪmjəˈleɪʃn/ n a situation in which real-life conditions are created on a computer in order to study or experience something

sketch /sketʃ/ v to draw quickly and simply without details

smart /smɑːt/ adj capable of intelligent action; equipped with a processor

smoke detector /ˈsməʊk dɪˌtektə(r)/ n a safety device which provides warning of smoke

software /ˈsɒftweə(r)/ n the programs that control the operation of a computer

sound system /ˈsaʊnd ˌsɪstəm/ n equipment for playing recorded or live music and for making it louder

sound-proofed /ˈsaʊndpruːfd/ adj made so that sound cannot get out

spray /spreɪ/ v to force out liquid in very small drops under pressure

stick /stɪk/ v to attach something firmly to something else using adhesive

storey /ˈstɔːri/ n a level or floor of a building

stressed /stresd/ adj subjected to a force per unit area that tends to change the dimensions of the material

stretch /stretʃ/ v to make something become wider or longer, for example by pulling it

structure /ˈstrʌktʃə(r)/ n something which is made up of many parts, especially a building

subject /ˈsʌbdʒekt/ n an area of study

suction /ˈsʌkʃn/ n the process of

removing air in order to create a partial vacuum

supervise /ˈsuːpəvaɪz/ *v* to be in charge of something and make sure that everything is done correctly

supplies /səˈplaɪz/ *n* the parts and materials that a manufacturer needs to make things

support /səˈpɔːt/ *n* a part or structure that holds something firmly in position; help that a company offers to customers using its products

tagging /ˈtæɡɪŋ/ *n* a system where an electronic device is attached to a person in order to know where they are at all times

take-off /ˈteɪkɒf/ *n* the beginning of a flight, when a plane or spacecraft rises from the ground

technician /tekˈnɪʃn/ *n* a highly-skilled scientific or industrial worker

three-dimensional /ˌθriː daɪˈmenʃənl/ *adj* showing length, breadth, and height, giving a solid appearance

throttle /ˈθrɒtl/ *n* a valve that controls the flow of fuel to an engine

thrust /θrʌst/ *n* the forward moving power of an engine

track /træk/ *n* any of the pieces of music on a recording

traffic /ˈtræfɪk/ *n* the movement of vehicles along roads

training /ˈtreɪnɪŋ/ *n* the process of learning the skills needed to do a job

trend /trend/ *n* the general direction in which something is changing or developing

trigger /ˈtrɪɡə(r)/ *n* a small metal lever that you press with your finger to fire a gun

two-dimensional /ˌtuː daɪˈmenʃənl/ *adj* showing only length and height or breadth; represented on a flat piece of paper

two-stroke /ˈtuː strəʊk/ *adj* an engine which requires two piston strokes per crankshaft revolution

ultrasound /ˈʌltrəsaʊnd/ *n* high-frequency sound

unique /juːˈniːk/ *adj* the only one of its type; not like any other

unmanned /ˌʌnˈmænd/ *adj* having no people on board

update /ʌpˈdeɪt/ *v* to get the most recent version of something

valve /vælv/ *n* a device which controls the flow of a fluid

vary /ˈveəri/ *v* to be different from one situation, model, etc. to the next

vertical /ˈvɜːtɪkl/ *adj* standing upright, at 90°

vibrate /vaɪˈbreɪt/ *v* to move from side to side very quickly and with small movements

virtual /ˈvɜːtʃʊəl/ *adj* that exists only in a computer, not in real life

virus /ˈvaɪrəs/ *n* instructions hidden in a computer program that are designed to cause faults or destroy data

voice-operated /ˌvɔɪs ˈɒpəreɪtɪd/ *adj* that can be made to work using only spoken instructions

wear /weə(r)/ *n* damaging effects of ordinary use over a long period

wear /weə(r)/ *v* to damage something by using it over a long period

web page /ˈweb peɪdʒ/ *n* an individual page of information on the Internet

welding /ˈweldɪŋ/ *n* the joining of like materials by heat

wireless hotspot /ˌwaɪələs ˈhɒtspɒt/ *n* a place, in a hotel or restaurant, etc., fitted with a special device that enables you to connect a computer to the Internet without using wires

OXFORD
UNIVERSITY PRESS

Great Clarendon Street, Oxford OX2 6DP

Oxford University Press is a department of the University of Oxford.
It furthers the University's objective of excellence in research, scholarship,
and education by publishing worldwide in

Oxford New York

Auckland Cape Town Dar es Salaam Hong Kong Karachi
Kuala Lumpur Madrid Melbourne Mexico City Nairobi
New Delhi Shanghai Taipei Toronto

With offices in

Argentina Austria Brazil Chile Czech Republic France Greece
Guatemala Hungary Italy Japan Poland Portugal Singapore
South Korea Switzerland Thailand Turkey Ukraine Vietnam

OXFORD and OXFORD ENGLISH are registered trade marks of
Oxford University Press in the UK and in certain other countries

ISBN: 978 0 19 4569507

Printed in China

ACKNOWLEDGEMENTS

Source: p.10 Full-time prospectus, Edinburgh's Telford College

*The authors and publisher are grateful to the following for their permission to reproduce
photographs and illustrative material*: AbioMed p.74 (artificial heart); Adidas p.26
(Adidas 1 trainers); Alamy Images pp.5 (old computer/Index Stock), 11 (lecture
hall chairs/D.Hurst), 14 (car production line/David Ball), 24 (kayak/Yadid Levy),
40 (bakery/Profimedia International s.r.o.), 40 (bakery/Profimedia International
s.r.o.), 49 (quad bike/Mike Greenslade), 49 (microlite/Steve Sant), 80 (man in
bath/Andy Bishop), 92 (broadcast cars/Gari Wyn Williams), 92 (DAB radio/
Joe Tree), 92 (video mobile call/CoverSpot); Corbis pp.4 (car by lake/Martyn
Goddard), 5 (doctor/Steve Prezant), 7 (Apple display/Kim Kulish), 14 (chemical
technician/William Taufic), 14 (shipyard/TWPhoto), 16 (man drilling/Jim
Craigmyle), 16 (car interior/Sagel & Kranefeld/zefa), 20 (red chairs/Jim Vecchi),
20 (turquoise chairs/Benjamin Rondel), 21 (Giorgetto Giugiaro/Vittorio Rastelli),
22 (biker/Roy McMahon), 23 (bike mechanic/Stockbyte), 24 (pole vault/Randy
Faris), 24 (bobsleigh/Tin De Waele/Isisport), 24 (hang-glider/Geoff Kalt/zefa),
29 (man with radio/Gideon Mendel), 40 (bread factory worker/Heinz

Wedewardt/zefa), 46 (Road Train/Christine Osborne), 46 (space shuttle carrier),
49 (Mars explorer NASA/epa), 52 (swimmer Paul Miller/epa), 70 (construction
workers/Charles C. Ebbets/Bettmann), 75 (pacemaker/Charles O'Rear), 80
(man with CDs/Parque/Zefa), 83 (Grand Theft Auto/Rockstar Games/Reuters),
86 (woman adjusting thermostat/Steve Chenn), 98 (technician examining
piping/Ted Horowitz), 98 (recording studio/Markus Moellenberg/zefa), 98
(agricultural engineer/Charles E. Rotkin), 100 (oil rig/Justin Guarigilia), 105
(radio programme/Despotovic Dusko/Sygma), 106 Wakamaru robot/Toshiyuki
Aizawa/Reuters); EA Games p.83 (Sims2); Empics Ltd p.94 (mobile phone
payment/Itsuo Inouye/AP); Epson pp.106 (inkjet technology), 111 (scanner),
112 (printer); Getty Images pp.4 (rocket launch/PicturePress/Photonica), 4
(mobile phone/Business Wire), 4 (coal power station/Jeremy Walker/Stone),
4 (laundry/Wide Group/Iconica), 5 (teacher/Ryan McVay/Taxi), 8 (Ariane 5
launch/AFP/Stringer), 8 (Proton launch/AFP/Stringer), 10 (young man smiling/
Peter Mason/Image Bank), 10 (students on steps/Marc Rohan), 14 (generator
turbine/Michael Melford/Image Bank), 16 (man drinking/Stock4B), 20 (cinema
chair/Dave Bradley/Taxi), 20 (classroom chairs/Superstudio/Iconica), 21 (Alec
Issigonis/Keystone), 34 (policeman/Peter Dazeley/Photographer's Choice), 35
(suitcase/Nicholas Veasey/Photographer's Choice), 36 (man wearing glasses/
Muntz/Image Bank), 46 (bullet train/Adastra/Taxi), 46 (Chinook helicopter/
Arnulf Husmo/Stone), 48 (man in office/Jean Louis Batt/Photographer's Choice),
52 (speed skater/Mike Powell/Allsport Concepts), 68 (Hong Kong skyline/
Asger Carlsen/Stone+), 69 (construction worker/Lester Lefkowitz), 72
(Sydney skyline/Davit Noton/Photographer's Choice), 76 (robot doctor/
Daniel Berehulak), 78 (ultrasound scanner/Business Wire), 84 (mobile phone/
Altrendo), 85 (Gran Turismo demonstration/Toshifumi Kitamura), 92 (satellite/
Benjamin Shearn/Taxi), 92 (man watching TV/Pankaj & Insy Shah/Gulfimages),
101 (young woman/Nick Dolding/Taxi), 103 (executives with score cards/Noel
Hendrickson/Riser), 112 (widescreen monitor/Business Wire); HP p.94 (iPaq);
Intelligent Energy p.48 (hydrogen bike); Logitech pp.111 (mouse, speakers,
webcam), 112 (VoIP phone, gamepad); Masterfile p.5 (shopkeeper/Ron Fehling);
Muji p.20 (CD player); OLPC p.30 (wind-up laptop); OUP pp.8 (smoke detector/
Hemera), 24 (baseball bat/Hemera), 24 (football/Hemera), 24 (ski poles/Hemera),
24 (tennis racket/Hemera), 24 (skates/Hemera), 24 (helmet/Hemera), 34
(flashlight/Hemera), 34 (police vest/Hemera), 34 (gas can/Hemera), 34
(radio/Hemera), 40 (bicycle/Hemera), 40 (CD cases/Hemera), 93 (young man/
ImageSource), 93 (TV set/Hemera), 99 (bridge/Hemera), 99 (radio/Hemera),
99 (microphone/Hemera), 107 (telephone/Hemera), 108 (circuit board),
110 (skateboard/Hemera); Photolibrary.com pp.37 (antitheft tag/Jed Share
Photograph/Workbook), 98 (chemical engineer/Maximilian Stock Ltd), 98
(engineer/Cadaphoto/Stock4b); Pierre d'Alancaisez p.34 handcuffs; Professor
Stephen Salter p.53 (Dervish); Punchstock pp.5 (man with guitar/Johnîr), 7
(mouse and DNA/Tetra Images), 13 (IT class/Digital Vision), 14 (man at computer/
Ciaran Friffin/Stockbyte Platinum), 16 (man with backpack), 16 (can opener/
John Wilkes Studio), 16 (man wearing headphones), 19 (portrait/Digital Vision),
37 (security camera/PhotoDisc), 63 (man with camcorder/PhotoAlto), 64
technician), 70 (construction site workers/StockByte), 78 (CAT scanner/IT
stock free), 80 (girl listening to music/Rubberball), 81 (interviewee/ImageSource),
82 (portrait/Digital Vision), 86 (barcode scanner), 86 (woman using computer
in library/Blend), 89 (woman wearing headset at computer/StockByte), 90
(downloading reflection/Blend), 97 (Space Shuttle/PhotoDisc), 98 (prosthetics
technician/PhotoDisc); Punchstock/Veer (cover image); Rex Features pp.21
(Philippe Starck), 29 (Trevor Baylis), 49 (Watercar), 49 (woman on Segway),
50 (JCB Dieselmax), 62 (telesurgery/Voisin/Phanie), 86 (military control room),
113 (E-ink); Rotundus p.38 (security ball); Science Photo Library pp14 (aircraft
technician/Maximilian Stock Ltd), 46 (electric car)

Illustrations by: Army of Trolls/NB Illustration (Customer care features),
Graham White/NB Illustration (pp.29, 30, 31, 42, 43, 44, 47, 53, 56–59, 61, 72,
74, 87, 96, 112, 113) and Ian Whadcock/Eastwing (pp.6, 12, 19, 24, 25, 28, 30,
32, 36, 42, 48, 54, 55, 71, 83, 88, 95, 102, 104)

Special thanks are due to: Norman Glendinning, Neil Foreman BEng (Hons) MBA